FINDING YOUR BASHERT

Strategies For Success

BY SHANI STEIN

THE JUDAICA PRESS
1999

Library of Congress Cataloging-in-Publication Data

Stein, Shani.
Finding Your Bashert: The Essential Guide to Finding the Perfect Mate
by Shani Stein
p. cm.
ISBN 1-880582-34-1
1. Mate selection—Religious aspects—Judaism.
2. Dating (Social customs)—Religious aspects—Judaism.
3. Man-woman relationships—Religious aspects—Judaism.   I. Title.
BM713.S74   1999
646.7'7'089924—dc21   CIP 99-25994

THE JUDAICA PRESS, INC.
123 Ditmas Avenue
Brooklyn, New York 11218
718-972-6200   800-972-6201
JudaicaPr@aol.com
www.judaicapress.com

Manufactured in the United States of America

Harav Dovid Goldwasser
Khal Bais Yitzchok
Brooklyn, NY

הרב דוד גאלדוואסער
קהל בית יצחק
ברוקלין, ניו יורק

בס"ד
ראש חודש שבט

"זיווגו של אדם קשה בקריאת ים סוף"

Our Chazal tell us that bringing about a shidduch is as difficult as the splitting of the Red Sea.

Every shidduch happens through *nissim*, miracles, hidden and revealed. In the same way that *Kriyas Yam Suf* occurred with great *nissim v'niflaos*, so too, every shidduch is laden with miracles.

When Eliezer went to secure a shidduch for Yitzchak, we learn that the earth came toward him; meaning that Eliezer was able to reach his destination supernaturally, in a fraction of the usual time.

The *Chiddushei Harim* questions the necessity of a supernatural occurrence. Eliezer could still have made the journey although it may have taken additional time. He answered that this was to show all future generations that every shidduch comes about through miracles.

There is an important lesson to be learned from this idea. Many people who are currently seeking their *zivug*, who have gone through difficult times, begin to wonder whether they will ever find who they are looking for. They begin to get upset and become somewhat disillusioned. What the great *Chiddushei Harim* tells us, is never give in to feelings of despair. In the world of shidduchim, miracles happen. There is a *zivug* for every person in the world; we need only to keep our *emunah* strong and to daven.

With this second book, Miss Shani Stein illuminates and clarifies many issues concerning shidduchim. She is a מזכה את הרבים who sincerely unites her considerable כוחות and talents to be a source of strength and encouragement for אחינו בני ישראל. As we learn from Chazal, דברה תורה בלשון בני אדם—the Torah sometimes employs the language best understood by the common man. Miss Stein has written this book in her own unique style which can be easily read by people from various backgrounds. As her first book was so widely well received, so too, will this much needed volume no doubt meet with the same enthusiastic success.

May Miss Stein's work always find חן בעיני אלקים ואדם.

With a humble תפילה to the Ribbono Shel Olam that our בקשות for זיווגים are accepted on high and that every *mishpacha* in Klal Yisroel share, בשורות טובות, ישועות ונחמות!

המצפה לישועה,

Rav Dovid Goldwasser

DEDICATED TO

my father

who has taught me the real meaning

of pursuing one's dreams and

maintaining one's Torah commitment at all costs.

TABLE OF CONTENTS

ACKNOWLEDGEMENTS

I would like to thank everyone who has put in their time, effort and genuine concern to make sure that this book is as successful as my first book. These are the people who cared to share the experiences felt by single people everywhere and to improve their situation. First, I'd like to thank the rabbis who guided me and kept me on track with the Torah perspective on all the ideas I came up with: Rabbi Dovid Goldwasser, my rav and advisor, Rabbi Abromchik, a successful shadchan from Chicago who has a real understanding of the intricacies of shidduchim, and Rabbi Leeb Kelleman from Neve Yerushalayim who always inspires me to goodness. A special thanks to Rachel Markowitz, a terrific shadchan who lent her clever insight to many issues in this book.

Then there are my wonderful friends whom I cannot thank

enough: Miriam Piamenta once again showed me the humor in every situation; Chaya Eisenberg lent her insights on *bitachon* and *hishtadlus*; Rachelly Solomon shared her terrific sense of style; Ayala Ovits gave me down-to-earth, practical advice; Sherry Feller shared her excellent ideas; Esti Whidekehr, helped with the *Ma'amarei Chazal*. Many thanks also to Tehilla Azar for being one of the most resourceful people I know; Martin Bodek, for his beautiful poem; Maxine Freedman, a relationship consultant (phone number: 617-730-5775), for her endless guidance and deep insight into all areas related to shidduchim. In addition I'd like to thank the many other friends who have helped but prefer to remain anonymous—I thank you all so much for helping me with this project.

My family has been wonderful as usual. My father, my mother, my sisters Chaya and Dassi, my brothers Duvi and Eli, my Bobby and Zeidy Stein and my Bobby and Zeidy Reichman —I'd like to thank each of them individually. They are my cheering squad and I have learned that having a mother, father, siblings, and grandparents who support my dreams is perhaps one of the most important things in the world.

And then, of course, there is the Judaica Press staff. Specifically I would like to thank Bonnie Goldman for editing and shaping the book, and Barbara Weinblatt and Zisi Berkowitz for all of their help. I gave them a book and they turned it into a masterpiece. They left no detail unaccounted for. Everything from the editing to the typesetting was done with meticulous care—thank you for helping me make this work!

INTRODUCTION

S ome of you may be curious about what happened to my
dating life after I wrote *The Survival Guide to Shidduchim.* Perhaps you imagine, "She probably had dates who
said, 'Whatever happens on this date, make sure I'm not chapter five of your next book!'" Maybe other guys had the book
hidden under their seat and discretely referred to it during the
date to make sure they were doing things right.

Well, if you are really curious, someone did ask me not to
turn him into a chapter and I assured him that our date was "off
the record." But, *boruch Hashem,* for the most part, my life
after writing *The Survival Guide to Shidduchim* has been
good. Yet, of course, there were times after I wrote my first
book when I considered changing my name so that I would not
have to go through the same *shpiel* each time somebody asked

me who I was. "Oh! *You* are Shani Stein—you must be the girl who wrote *The Survival Guide to Shidduchim*." I considered

> **I wrote the book to help give people an upbeat, optimistic outlook about shidduchim.**

saying, "Shani Stein? Who's that? My name is Shprintze Rosenblum—my favorite pastime is washing dishes!"

The truth is, *The Survival Guide to Shidduchim* not only made life more interesting, it also made my life fun—make that really fun. Writing the book gave me the chance to meet so many interesting people whose lives would have never crossed with mine under ordinary circumstances. Apart from this, I wrote the book to help give people an upbeat, optimistic outlook about shidduchim. And I considered the book a success, if I made even one hermit living on an island near the Bermuda Triangle chuckle while he was reading it. Many people told me that the book gave them something to talk about on their dates. One friend of mine said that thanks to my book, she doesn't suffer from conversation shortages any more. She says every time she's out with a guy and the conversation goes dead, a *bas kol* comes out of the sky and says, "We're experiencing a lull. It'll be over shortly. Thanks to the advice I received in Shani's book, it will definitely be over shortly."

This book includes everything I left out of *The Survival Guide to Shidduchim*. This book has an entirely new focus, yet it can and should be read by everyone who is in the shidduch parshah. Its focus is twofold: the sophisticated or "seasoned" dater as I call it and the parents of shidduch daters.

When I refer to the sophisticated dater, I am referring to someone who has been dating for a while and has become a little (or a lot!) jaded or tired. They may feel as if they have dated everyone in the Western hemisphere. Every time a new name is mentioned to them they sigh because they have already gone out or checked into the individual and are pretty sure that he or she is not for them.

In my first book I mentioned that it is almost impossible to change another person. However *you* have unlimited abilities to change from within. It is totally within the realm of possibility to change yourself and your attitudes about dating. Anyone can begin dating in a more focused, effective way and head their dating life in a totally new direction. Instead of thinking whenever you go on a date: "Here goes another one! I'm waiting for this guy/girl to impress *me*!" this book will hopefully teach you how to become more animated and enthusiastic about your dates.

When I tell people to have fun on their dates, their typical response is, "How can I have fun when everything I say is being scrutinized, every gesture analyzed, every article of clothing inspected!" This attitude will only lead to panic! You want to work on abolishing this attitude. Try to incorporate a new positive dating outlook so that instead of going into each date thinking, "I'd rather be out with friends," you—the sophisticated dater with the new attitude—will go into every date calm and at ease, prepared to give every single person you go out with a fair chance.

The second focus of this book is the parents of shidduch daters. After talking to many parents, I was amazed to discover that it is altogether possible that parents have it harder than their children when it comes to shidduchim! To be a parent (so I am told) means your children's successes are your successes, their dreams are your dreams and believe it or not—sometimes their dating life becomes your dating life. In some cases, this is so extreme that parents who have daughters, for instance, can be seen becoming noticeably more tense and anxious as the hour that the boy is supposed to arrive draws near. Many mothers become instant neat freaks and are at the coffee table with their Windex bottles scrubbing it till it's shiny. Many fathers, though usually the more relaxed of the two, can be seen pacing back and forth making sure all the little kids are well hidden. Many parents could use a good dose of coaching as well.

To help guide parents, I aimed myself in two directions. I first interviewed parents concerning how they felt they should and shouldn't be interacting with their children during the dating process. I then went to people in the process of dating and asked how they felt their parents could help make their lives easier. Once I understood how the two different sides felt about the issue, I proceeded to write one unified perspective that could work for both sides.

I hope you enjoy this book and discover useful ideas and answers. I hope this book helps you adopt a more productive, optimistic outlook about the dating process and puts you in the right frame of mind to meet your bashert soon. Enjoy!

FINDING YOUR BASHERT

Strategies For Success

BREAKING DOWN THE BARRIERS PREVENTING YOU FROM GETTING MARRIED

We can all name someone who has dated hundreds of people and woke up ten years later wondering where all the time went. For some reason or another they failed to find their bashert. Perhaps they erected too many barriers while they were dating and, in essence, chased people away. Or perhaps they were scared of really finding someone. A growing segment of the Jewish single population is slipping into their late 20's and 30's and wants to know: a) What is preventing them from getting married? And once they know this, b) What can they do to eliminate these barriers?

This chapter will help give you some ideas about what may be stopping *you* from getting married. If you have just begun dating, this chapter will identify the ideal dating mind set which will help you find your bashert sooner rather than later.

Let's first acknowledge that dating is stressful. The experience of dating over many years can cause someone to feel burnt

> **The time you are to be married is all written in G-d's master-plan book.**

out and discouraged with the whole dating scene. One may begin to feel that, G-d forbid, there is no one out there for them. People who have been dating for ten years or more often express disillusionment. They ask, "Where did I go wrong?" While the time you are to be married is all written in G-d's master-plan book, there is an element of *hishtadlus* as well as *bitachon* that comes into play (see chapter 8).

You might be better equipped to face and eventually altogether eliminate these obstacles if you have some clear notion of the obstacles stopping you from getting married. It will take some introspection to discover why you keep on saying "No," to guys or girls who could potentially make excellent spouses.

I am a firm believer that self-knowledge is the key to finding happiness. When you go into shul, and you feel the stares, and read the expressions on people's faces, "Nuuu, so what's taking you so long?" all it does is make you more nervous. But if you had the necessary information that would allow you to reflect on why it is taking you so long to find someone, you would then be able to work at changing the situation.

So get a pen (I'll wait!) and prepare yourself to answer some very eye-opening questions. It may seem like a silly exercise but you'll find that thinking theses things through will be helpful. Don't worry if some of the items on this list apply and others are completely off the mark—this is just a helpful tool to begin the process of self-examination.

1. Are You Confusing Your Needs With Your Wants?

Ask yourself the following questions:

What do I really *need* from a spouse? What do I *want* from a spouse? Please try to list these items in order of importance, with the most important item #1, etc.

NEEDS	WANTS

The Difference Between Needs & Wants

You may be wondering what exactly is the difference between something you *need* and something you *want*. Well, a "need" is something that you have really thought about and something that you are *sure* you can't live without. Under this category should be things like, "someone who has a good

> **Remember, to find anything, you need to know what you are looking for and what you need.**

heart," "someone who will take his religious commitment seriously," "someone who is authentically interested in learning," or even "someone who is easygoing," "someone who is generous" or "someone who is considerate." Please take your time and really think about this.

Remember, to find *anything*, you need to know *what* you are looking for and what you need. (To do this exercise you may have to do some serious soul-searching!) For this list please consider only what *you* need and *not* what your parents or friends may need!

A "want," on the other hand, is something that it would be nice to have. Under this category you will find the specific personality types you may be looking for such as, "I want the life-of-the-party type," or "I want someone tall and handsome or blonde and petite." You might also find things like, "I want to live in Israel one day" and "I want someone who shares my love of music." If you keep in mind what you cannot live with-

4

out as opposed to what would be nice, you may eliminate some of the confusion involved in finding a spouse. Without doing this important work you'll probably have problems choosing a mate. Remember dating involves picking a life mate—it takes a lot of thought to figure out what you think you need for a lifetime of contentment. Think about how much shopping and research you may do for the right dress or suit or car!

Choosing a spouse will take a lot of preparatory work— you'll need to know yourself well enough to know what kind of person you need! Once you've completed your list of what you're looking for in a spouse, it may help to post your list in your room to ensure that you stay focused as you date. It's easy to get distracted as you meet new people. You don't want to trade off something you value as a priority for something that is a passing fancy.

2. Are You Insecure About What You Can Offer Someone In A Marriage?

Many people, unfortunately, believe that a) they are unworthy of anybody or b) nobody will like them.

It may not be a conscious feeling. It may just be below the surface. Someone with low self-esteem may say "no" to many possible matches in order to prevent themselves from getting hurt. Someone like this will think that if they really like someone and then this person is not interested, they will be devastated by the rejection. So instead they purposely avoid dating people they are really interested in. These are detrimental and self-destructive feelings!

If this sounds even a little like you, then you need to work on your self-esteem. Self-esteem can be defined as, "I like me;" in other words—belief in oneself. People are naturally drawn to others who like themselves and display self-confidence. While you are dating you will need to become your own cheering squad and learn to appreciate the qualities that make you a terrific person. You will need to learn how to project self-confidence—even if you yourself are not completely convinced. (How are you going to get others to like you if you aren't convinced you're likeable?)

Even if it feels awkward, write down five things that you like about yourself:

1. _____ 2. _____ 3. _____

4. _____ 5. _____

Hopefully, you've had no trouble filling out at least five items! Although it may feel embarrassing to do this, it really helps to remember the things you value in yourself in order to build your confidence. If you acknowledge things you like in yourself, there is no question that you will find someone else who will also like these things.

Remember that each one of us has a tremendous amount to offer. Each of us has unique talents: whether it's a sharp mind, artistic talent, humorous point of view, mathematical ability, organizing skill, conversational aptitude, etc. Some people are great listeners, some are born givers. Everyone has strengths. There is no such thing as not having something to offer some-one else in a marriage.

> **What makes someone interesting and attractive is their sense of self— their self-confidence, and their peaceful contentment with who they are and how they look!**

If you're the one people talk to when they are feeling down, or you're the guy people always take shopping because you have a great sense of style, or maybe you keep calm even when the house is tumbling down around you—these are qual-ities that you should learn to appreciate in yourself. Because if you don't appreciate *you*, why should you expect another per-son to appreciate you? Think about the people you know and like—examine what it is that makes them so likeable. You'll notice that often what makes someone interesting and attractive is their own sense of self—their self-confidence, their peaceful contentment with who they are and how they look!

I know you've already made yourself a list of what you want in a spouse. Now it's time to make yourself a "give" list. Write down ten things you feel you can offer someone in a marriage:

1. _____   6. _____

2. _____   7. _____

3. _____   8. _____

4. _____   9. _____

5. _____   10. _____

I hope this exercise has helped you see that you are indeed a talented, special person who is worthy of being loved. It's important to project to others that you are content and that you are happy with who you are. Remember you're in the "market" for a shidduch and sometimes you need to be well aware of your "selling points!" If you find that you are having problems filling this out—perhaps you can ask a good friend to help!

3. Are You Afraid Of Getting Hurt?

Many people who have been dating for a while (and even some who haven't) are afraid of allowing themselves to feel any positive emotion for the person they are dating. It's as if they have enclosed their emotions in an iron cage and refuse to release them. It may be related to a previous experience when they let their emotions go and allowed themselves to open up and feel something for another person. Then they were rejected and ended up feeling hurt (it could be this happened long ago when they were a little kid or it may have happened more recently).

> **Are you scared of getting into a serious relationship with someone because you are afraid you will get hurt if he or she rejects you?**

We are like small, fragile glass figurines—we easily break. We expend so much effort in preserving our pride or ego that when it gets stamped on one time too many, we may end up building a cement wall around ourselves so that we will never be hurt again.

Ask yourself honestly: Are you scared of getting into a seri-

8

ous relationship with someone because you are afraid you will get hurt if he or she rejects you?

Unfortunately, the reality is that one has to be a little vulnerable when dating. Dating is sharing who you are with someone else. When you "play hard to get" you only hurt yourself. This is a difficult reality, but something that it's best to acknowledge.

Getting Close to Someone
Involves Taking Emotional Risks

Rabbi Kelleman from Neve Yerushalayim taught me that in life we must be our own advocate. We have to have the guts to proceed and accomplish what we want in life. And clearly it does take courage and strength to take risks!

Rabbi Kelleman once relayed to me an apropos story: Rabbi Kelleman is a talmid of Rav Shlomo Wolbe, from Yerushalayim. For many years, when he was younger, he attended a shiur given by Rav Wolbe exclusively for him and four other bochorim at the yeshivah. Rabbi Kelleman's eyes would mist over when he talked about how much he loved Rav Wolbe and how he enjoyed these semi-private weekly shiurim where he could ask Rav Wolbe anything and everything that was on his mind.

At one point, Rav Wolbe was inundated with responsibilities and had to stop this weekly shiur. One night he came into the classroom and announced that the Tuesday night 8:00 p.m. shiur would be canceled, although they were welcome to attend his Monday night shiur given to the general public.

Rabbi Kelleman was devastated. How was he ever going to speak to his beloved Rav Wolbe when there were 200 people standing on line to ask him questions?!

The following Tuesday night Rabbi Kelleman completely forgot that his shiur with Rav Wolbe had been canceled and he went to the Bais Medrash anyway. He walked up the steps of the building and when he came to the room where the shiur was usually held he noticed that the room was dark and deserted. He immediately remembered that the Rav had canceled the shiur and this triggered in him a heavy feeling of despair. He walked into the dark classroom, took a seat and began to cry.

He was crying to himself for some time when he heard the door open. He turned around and there was Rav Wolbe walking toward him. Rav Wolbe saw his tears and asked him, "What's wrong, my son?" Rabbi Kelleman answered, "How will I ever get to speak to you in that large crowd? Who will I turn to for answers to my questions? I can't live without your guidance." Rav Wolbe turned to his beloved talmid and said, "Come to the shiur Monday night and everything will be okay."

The following Monday night, Rabbi Kelleman came to the public shiur and took his seat amidst the sea of people. After Rav Wolbe's incredible shiur had ended he was filled with questions for the Rav. He ran up to the shtender as quickly as possible to be first on the line to speak to him.

Unfortunately, by the time he got there, there were already at least fifty people in front of him on line. He waited and waited for his turn to come. He began to feel increasingly discouraged. Suddenly, from the middle of the crowd came a shuffling of movement. Rabbi Kelleman saw Rav Wolbe from the far distance waving a finger in his direction. The enormous crowd of people split like the Red Sea in front of Rabbi Kelleman. "Me?" he asked Rav Wolbe, pointing at himself—

> **The enormous crowd of people split like the Red Sea in front of Rabbi Kelleman. "Me?" he asked Rav Wolbe, pointing at himself.**

sure that the Rav couldn't possibly want him out of this gigantic crowd of people. The Rav nodded his head. The huge crowd of people parted down the center and everyone stood back as Rabbi Kelleman walked forward. He asked the Rav all his questions about the shiur as well as about anything else that had come up during the week and the Rav listened and gave him answers.

From that week on, every Monday night Rabbi Kelleman would go to the shiur and Rav Wolbe would always find the time to call him up privately to answer everything that was on Rav Kelleman's mind.

The story so moved me. Rabbi Kelleman taught me the importance of having the guts to accomplish what you need in life—which may involve revealing your true feelings and not allowing your fragile ego or silly pride get in the way. Had he not had the courage to reveal to Rav Wolbe exactly how he felt about losing him as a teacher and how much he needed him, he may never have had the continued private audience with him.

Each of us has to make sure we are in control of our lives and are unafraid to take risks to accomplish our goals and get what we need from life. We have to make sure we are not in the habit of running away from risky situations for fear we'll be hurt. (Of course, Hashem is the One Who really oversees our life; however, even under His Divine providence there is room for us to be in control of what is happening to us.) Looking for a shidduch is not the time for cowardliness or for useless worries about bruising one's ego. Rather, it is the time to start putting your ego on the line and trying to let go of your fears. Remember, it is our life to win and our life to lose, and we want to make sure that in the end we have no regrets!

4. Is It An Issue Of Commitment?

Fear of commitment is astonishingly common. The idea of being tied down in a committed relationship frightens many people. If this sounds like you, it may be that one of the obstacles preventing you from finding the right person is that you are truly scared of settling down. Possibly you have simply grown accustomed to your independence; perhaps you are secretly content with your present situation. Getting used to another person at this point in your life may feel scary. A fear of commitment may also be related to fear of rejection. Perhaps you fear investing your emotions in someone because you fear that as soon as you do so they'll reject you—so you avoid opening up and beginning the process of commitment.

If you recognize any or all of these feelings, you may be

experiencing a degree of "commitment phobia." One good question to ask yourself to be certain is:

Can you give yourself a specific date by which you would like to be married? If this question scares the living daylights out of you, then this may be a problem you need to look further at. If you feel relaxed about this question then it will be easy to do this exercise.

Target Marriage Date

Date: _____

Remember, if you can't commit to a certain date, you might have some degree of commitment phobia.

Another question you might want to ask yourself is:

Name three things preventing you from settling down *today*?

1. _____

2. _____

3. _____

If you are having absolutely no trouble filling up this list, and as a matter of fact you have already added a #4, #5 and #6, it may be that you are actually not ready to commit to someone at this point of your life even if you feel convinced that you are ready. Or perhaps you're simply afraid to take a risk—perhaps you reject people to *protect* yourself from getting rejected!

While you are dating, it is important to identify which track you are on. Are you on the "noncommittal" track where you say "no" to individuals left and right without really giving them a fair chance? Do you find little things wrong with each person you date? Or, are you on the "marriage" track, where every single person you go out with is given a fair chance—and you begin each date with the underlying belief: this could be the right person. If you find yourself on the "noncommittal" track, it is important to become aware of this pattern early on and, with the help of a trusted rabbi, a wise married friend, or even a psychotherapist, begin chipping away at this attitude. Because if you don't do something about this now, you'll just stand in place and never progress in your goal to get married.

One thing you can do which might help is to sit down with a close married friend and discuss the benefits of marriage. This should be done with a person whose marriage you admire—someone who can give you specific reasons why marriage is great. Perhaps you don't even realize it but you may have a negative image of marriage. Really talking to a happily married person may give you a clear sense of why you want to be married and how good it can be for you personally.

5. Playing The Comparing Game.

It is natural to want to find a spouse you'll be proud of. But this could go too far! Other people's opinions should *not* take precedence! Ask yourself the following question:

Do you find yourself comparing your dates to your friends' dates or spouses before you even know your date?

If the answer is yes, then possibly this is one thing that may be hindering your search. Only *you* need to be satisfied with your spouse. Many of us

> **Keep in mind that only <u>you</u> need to be satisfied with your spouse.**

feel the need to measure our accomplishments and possessions against those of others around us.

Yes, there are some confident people out there who can honestly say they are unaffected by people's opinions but, for most of us, this is a distant reality. We look at our friends' cars, homes, jobs, and salaries and, sadly, think it's important that we match those around us. Although we are happy with other's successes, all the while we wonder if what we have measures up. However, keep in mind that what makes your friend happy, would, in many cases, not work for you at all.

Alternatively, the person who will be right for you, and would make you excited to be alive, will be someone who completes *you*—not your neighbor, relative or friend. Therefore, all efforts at comparison will be harmful to your best interest. This takes self-awareness—and the hard work of getting to know yourself—but only *you* know your priorities and what you desire in a spouse. Maybe you don't really care what kind of car your husband will drive even if your friend thinks this is important! Or maybe it's unimportant whether your wife has blue eyes! Each of us is unique and we each need to find a spouse that will please only us. It may take some courage but it is your choice who you consider your bashert.

Do You Compare Your Dates To Each Other?

After your dates, do you find yourself thinking, "if only he had Chaim's personality and Yaakov's looks and Dov's job but still had those twinkling eyes, he would be perfect"? Or "if only she had Miriam's smile, Chaya's personality and Zisi's money"?

If the answer is yes, this is a key pattern to identify in yourself and work at removing. The basic premise here is: You will *never* find someone perfect. Not now, not tomorrow, not ever!

Many women want to find someone with the looks of Yosef Hatzadik, the money of Rav Yehudah Hanasi and the brilliance of Rabbi Akiva. Men want someone who looks like a Hollywood starlet even when she just woke up in the morning, cooks like Betty Crocker, and keeps a house like Martha Stewart. He/she is not out there—that's it! Discussion is over!

You need to prioritize—it's helpful to go through the first exercise in this chapter and make a list of the top five items crucial to making *you* content. Eventually, G-d will give us someone who is perfect for us. With this person one will be able to achieve one's highest potential as a human being. It is by growing together and coming to accept our life partner's faults and idiosyncrasies that we develop and become a better person. If the person was handed to us exactly as we would like him or her to be—in essence a perfect, complete package with no assembly required—we'd never have the opportunity to grow.

The bottom line is one must not feel one is settling if one ends up with someone perfect for them but missing some of the qualities they may have originally hoped for. It will be impossible to find someone who fits all your criteria perfectly. Your goal is to find someone with whom you will be able to grow and fulfill your potential in life. If you find someone you authentically enjoy being with, someone who has similar values and goals, and with whom you have many things in common that should be sufficient—and it's rare to find even that!

It's not productive to compare your dates to one another in an effort to create the ideal being; stop playing "design-a-spouse" and start seeing your dates as a possible friend and life partner with whom you will have the exciting challenge of growing and working and becoming something better in the process.

6. Are You Unsure About Your Dates, Because They Don't Give You A Giddy, Excited Feeling That You've Heard People Say That They Experienced When They Found Their Bashert?

First of all this giddy, excited feeling may not mean very much. The most important criteria in choosing a partner is finding someone you really like and who has similar values and goals.

Answer this question about yourself: Are you a perpetual doubter?

Are you the type of person who has difficulty making decisions and changes your mind 50 times in the process?

Many people will doubt their decision no matter *who* they date, sometimes even if it is someone who is precisely who they have been looking for. These people have difficulty feeling completely at ease with their decisions, especially one as big as who they will ultimately marry. They may not feel that "giddy" feeling when they finally meet someone who is precisely who they have been looking for and thus may question if perhaps this person is the wrong one. They will wonder, "Is this rush of excitement in me not happening because he/she is wrong for me, or because I perpetually doubt decisions I make and thus have difficulty letting my emotions go?"

Even though we all expect to be charged up and dizzy with excitement when we meet the right person, the more cerebral among us—those who always need everything to make sense and be logical—may not get any heady feeling at all! While some charge of attraction is necessary for a relationship to work and you surely must enjoy being in this person's company, it's okay if you don't feel earthquakes whenever the two of you are together.

If you still need help identifying if you are a doubter type, ask yourself if you have trouble making small decisions, such as what to have for breakfast or which pair of shoes to buy or maybe what you'd like to do work-wise. And once you make a decision do you begin to think you may have made the wrong decision?

Maxine Freedman is a relationship specialist who has

tremendous intuition into all aspects of relationships, and who has helped me countless times when writing this book. She has been working with singles for thirteen years and has received part of her training from professional shadchanim in Israel. I asked her how one could "get better" or become less doubtful

> **Begin trusting your inner voice, your instincts—instead of what seems logical—and see what happens.**

about decisions. She suggested starting with a small decision, such as what you are going to eat for dinner. Begin trusting your inner voice, your instincts—instead of what seems logical—and see what happens.

Maybe you're just not used to doing something for yourself—something that makes just *you* feel good—and not your friends or relatives. A more advanced challenge would be to try to take care of your own needs even if it means missing out on fun with your friends.

Imagine, for instance, that you are exhausted and know that what you really need is a good night's sleep but your friends invite you to go to a concert. You know that the next day your friends will all be talking about the concert and you'll feel positively left out if you don't go. If you have the strength of will, however, you'll heed your body's voice and take that much needed night's sleep, you will feel rested in the morning and you'll have the confidence to face your friends the next day knowing you trusted your instinct and did the right thing for you. When you successfully master this exercise you will know that you are well on your way to being less indecisive and becoming someone who is more confident of making decisions.

Try to practice making and sticking with little decisions to help develop a stronger sense of will and realize the decisions you make are good for you. Some people say intuition is like G-d talking to you. The more you trust your intuition, the better you are able to make and stand by your decisions—such as sticking with someone you know is right for you.

7. Do You Say "No" To Many People Because Of A Physical Aspect Of The Person That Doesn't Attract You?

Ask yourself:

What was the main reason I said "no" to my last five dates?

1. _____

2. _____

3. _____

4. _____

5. _____

If you have filled in three or more of these spaces with something related to physical appearance, you might be suffering from the "super-model" syndrome (which, by the way, applies to guys as well as girls). A person's external appearance does *not* always reflect their internal state. They may be the most beautiful person externally, but on the inside lack a great deal. You'll realize how true this is when you think of people you really like and how beauti- ful they look to you because they are so sweet and lovely on the inside.

> **A person's external appearance does not always reflect their internal state. They may be the most beautiful person externally, but on the inside lack a great deal.**

Ask yourself if the physical characteristics which you feel are important, (i.e. height, hair color) make someone a good marriage partner. To find someone you can live with day in and day out you must look deeper. And if so, you'd acknowledge that you could still be happy with a man who was not six feet tall or blue eyed or, if you are a guy, you can still be content with someone even if they are not 5' 5", blonde and slender. Most of the physical characteristics which we may imagine are crucial to our happiness and the reasons we may be continually rejecting good marriage candidates, have absolutely no correlation with the happiness someone can bring to you in a marriage.

I heard an insightful story about a girl who went out with a guy for a long time. He felt she was everything he was looking for except for one small thing—she had a slight facial blemish. It bothered him so much that he approached his Rabbi and asked if he could ask the girl to have an operation to fix the problem. The Rabbi said he could. On their next date he approached the girl and confided how much he cared about her but how this one little thing drove him crazy. She agreed that after they married she would be happy to have the operation to remove the blemish.

Soon after they were married, with plans that she would have the operation a few months into the marriage. However, she became pregnant right away and the doctor felt it would be best if she waited to have the somewhat delicate operation, at least until after the baby was born. After her first baby was born she soon became pregnant again. Soon after the birth of her second child, she approached her husband and said, "I'm ready now for the operation." He turned to her, a confused expression on his face, and asked, "What operation?" She reminded him about the deal they had made. He responded, "I don't want you to get an operation. You're beautiful just the way you are!"—and he meant it.

It is difficult to tell how you will feel about a person's looks after you are married to them, but ask yourself, how important is a slightly long nose, or the wrong shade of hair, when your child has a fever, or when you have just been fired from your job? When the challenges of marriage present themselves, someone who is strong, confident and kindhearted will be the one you will want at your side.

8. Are You Scared Of Settling?

Ask yourself this question:

Do you fear settling for someone who is not exactly what you are looking for?

Before you can answer this question it may help to first

clarify exactly what we mean by "settling." Settling can be explained as accepting certain things in a spouse that you never thought you would. It takes some maturity to accept that life will not always be the way you would like it to be and sometimes you will have to adjust your expectations.

For example, perhaps it was unrealistic to think that you'd marry a doctor when you never went to college. The funny thing about maturity is that the older you get, the more mature you supposedly become, and yet many people find it increasingly harder to make a decision and choose someone to marry. They start to view life more rigidly and don't want to go for someone who would require them to make too many adjustments in their thinking or lifestyle. They say to themselves, "If I've waited this long, I can wait just a little longer till I find Mr. or Miss Right." It is the younger dating crowd, those more malleable and with less deeply ingrained beliefs, who are thus more likely to take someone who is completely different than they had expected and make the best of it. In essence, they are the ones who may be the most mature of all.

Chaya, for instance, was intent on marrying a medical school student, but she found a guy who was perfect in every way for her—except he was an accountant. She thought she was settling—but after they were married and she watched how little her friends saw their doctor husbands, she was absolutely gratified with her choice.

If settling means accepting what you will not be getting in a spouse and dealing with it in the best way, then it is simply a matter of realizing that, in life, the puzzle pieces often do not fit together perfectly and it takes more effort on one's part to see that they will eventually fit together smoothly.

Action Steps

Identify the barriers preventing you from getting married

1. Have you really considered what you need in the person you marry? Are you confusing your needs with your wants?

2. Are you insecure about what you can offer someone in a marriage?

3. Do you limit yourself because you are afraid of getting hurt?

4. Are you fearful of making a commitment?

5. Are you so busy wanting to impress others that you're not looking for what *you* truly need and want?

6. Are you unsure about choosing someone because they don't give you that giddy, excited feeling that your friends say that they experienced when they found their bashert?

7. Do you say "no" to many people because of a physical aspect of the person that does not attract you?

8. Are you scared of settling?

HOW DO I KNOW WHEN I'M ON THE RIGHT TRACK?

O nce you have done the hard work of establishing what, if any, are the barriers preventing you from getting married, you are ready to go out and find your soul mate.

According to John Gray, author *of Men Are From Mars, Women Are From Venus*, "a soul mate is someone who has the unique ability to bring out the best in us. Soul mates are not perfect, but they are perfect for us." The person you finally decide is your soul mate will most likely not have everything on your list of ideal qualities. However, they will have all the things you *need* to feel happy and good about yourself.

As I mentioned in the first chapter, one should prepare a list of no more then ten items they feel they need in a spouse. A guy or a girl should know if they definitely need someone who is learning, or if they'll need someone who will support them through learning, who can be their best friend, or who is very socially active, or who is communicative and affectionate. Each

> **There is an intuitive part to this. You really have to know who you are now, not who you want to be.**

of us has our own very specific list. There are certain things a dating individual cannot and should not compromise on. Through trial and error you will come to discover precisely the things you *need* vs. the things you would like to have.

There is an intuitive part to this. You really have to know who you are in order to know who would be right for you; you need to know what your strengths and weaknesses are—in essence, who you are now, *not* who you want to be.

Relationship consultant Maxine Freedman offered some advice on knowing if an individual is right for you: If, when going out with someone, you intuitively feel positive about the relationship and you are at a point where you feel "Yes! I think this is the one!"—take a step back and think of it instead as a "maybe" and be cautious as you gather more information about the person. If you have strong doubts, think of it instead as a no—for now. As you learn more about the person, and with the passage of time, you might come to see the person and the situation differently and be willing to give it another chance.

When you feel, "there's something about this relationship that's not right, but I can't put my finger on it,"—that's your intuition talking and it should be taken seriously. With time and practice you can become more and more in tune with what *your* intuition is telling you.

I asked Maxine (who is *B"H* happily married) what she felt were the signs to look for that would signal that you are in a good relationship and should stick with it. Together with her husband she came up with four excellent points:

Things To Look For

1. When you are not with this person, you miss them and think about them.

2. When you are together for a long duration—let's say four hours—it feels like you've been together only ten minutes.

3. When you have a conflict with this person, you are easily able to find a way to work it out.

4. You are compatible in terms of having similar long-term life goals.

This last point, though important for everyone, is particularly important in the religious world. People are often defined by their life goals and though it's true that people change over time, if a boy wants to learn in kollel, and the girl doesn't want this, they have quite different life goals. And do not for a minute think that you can ignore what your life goals have been. You do *not* want to commit to someone else's life goals—this can be a formula for disaster. Even at a young age we know what kind of home we want to have and we even may have some notion of the kind of life we would like to lead. Seeing eye to eye in this area with someone can be an excellent sign of compatibility.

A common problem I often hear is that when a guy or girl has finally found someone who has life goals similar to theirs, the person is missing something on their list. Should they pass on this person because of what's missing or stick with the person? Would it be settling not to keep looking?

This is incredibly difficult to answer. And for each person the answer is different. Before you can answer this question you have to clearly define what *you* consider trivial—those things that are nice but not necessary and can be written off as, "*lo chashuv*" or "not important," and thus looked past.

For instance, if you had your heart set on making *aliyah* to Israel within five years and the guy you are going out with does not think this is important, then this clearly is an important consideration. However, if you are a guy who always wanted to marry a blonde and she's a brunette, or if you are a girl who always wanted to marry someone tall with lots of hair and he's medium height and balding, that's "*lo chashuv*."

As they say, "keep your eye on the ball" or in other words, *stay focused*. In time it will get easier. And just remember, ten years down the road you won't even remember why you thought blonde hair or the other trivial detail was so important! Above all, don't even think you can marry someone because you like blondes, tall men, good-looking girls or some other trivial reason when you have totally different life goals and values—this is a guaranteed formula for disaster! Focus on things that count—like being compatible and being able to communicate and you'll be so much happier in the long run.

Good Relationships

Other experts on relationships offer other characteristics that will reveal to you if a relationship is worth holding on to:

1. You have to be comfortable sharing good things and bad things with the person.

2. The relationship is strong if you feel satisfied being supportive of the other person or sharing the tasks the other person may not enjoy doing—meaning you are willing to go out of your way for the other person.

> **Psychologists say that you will know that you really care for someone when the security and well-being of the other person becomes as significant as your own security and well being.**

3. Many psychologists say that you will know that you really care for someone when the security and well-being of the other person becomes as significant (not more significant) as your own security and well being.

4. Remember a marriage is made up of two people and must serve the spouses' mutual and individual needs. A good marriage will result from the caring and sensitive way you will treat each other. So if the person you're dating treats you with care and sensitivity then you're on the right path.

5. You know it's serious when you start thinking in terms of "we" instead of "I."

6. Another sign is when you would rather be with this person than with anyone else.

Good Personality Traits To Look For

1. Some people recommend choosing someone who is able or willing to adapt to the never-ending changes and circumstances of life relationships, i.e., someone resilient and not rigid.

2. A productive person is generally a happier person. And a happy person makes a good spouse. Find someone who has things they personally enjoy—whether it's a career or running a household.

3. Someone with the skills or awareness of how to maintain a good relationship is a better bet than someone with little awareness.

4. A good communicator makes a great spouse.

As you can see, finding a shidduch is serious business and will take a lot of work on your part. Once again, it will help immeasurably not to be alone in this process. Find a trusted rabbi, parent, or confidante to talk to—having someone you can really talk to will help you problem solve and keep you on the right track. After all, this is one of the most important decisions you can make and you want to make it for the right reasons.

Finally, you know you are on the right track if you are simply happy to be in the other person's presence and being around them makes you feel good. You need to enjoy just being with the person, because after all is said and done that's what's going to make your marriage successful. And you need to enjoy everyday events—like taking a walk or changing a tire or doing a chore—with this person and not just going to concerts, dinners and parties together. You want to be able to just enjoy sharing each other's company.

I asked a married friend of mine to answer the question, "How do I know if I'm settling in a relationship?" Her astute reply was: "If you broke up with him/her today, you would feel relieved not sorry."

Sometimes you'll find yourself dating someone for a while and you don't really have a reason for breaking it off, but you sort of wish they would. In essence you feel nothing is really wrong with them but nothing is very right either—that's a sign you're settling. You can't just be existing with this person but rather, there has to be something really right about it!

Action Steps

How you will know you've met someone who makes a good candidate for marriage:

1. When you are not with this person, you miss them and think about them.

2. When you are together for a long duration—let's say four hours—it feels like you've been together only ten minutes.

3. When you have a conflict about something with this person, you are able to find a way to work it out.

4. You are compatible in terms of having similar long-term life goals.

5. You are comfortable sharing good things and bad things.

6. You feel satisfied being supportive or sharing the tasks the other person may not enjoy doing—meaning you are willing to go out of your way for the other person.

THE SHIDDUCH WARDROBE—HOW TO DRESS FOR SUCCESS

No matter what anyone says—the first impression is important! Although it's crucial to enrich your soul and make yourself happier and a more interesting person, it's a reality that most people do judge a book by its cover. Clothing expresses a tremendous amount about a person. It reveals your personal style, who you want to be, and how you would like others to perceive you. It takes just two seconds for someone to visually take in your appearance and reach a first impression, so you want to make sure that you'll always look appealing and clean at first glance—and that you are conveying a clear message of who you are.

Believe it or not, the most important element in dressing well is cleanliness and neatness. Make sure you are showered and well groomed. Take a good look in the mirror each morning and make sure that your hair is neat, and all your clothes are crisp and clean and in absolutely *perfect* condition. If

> **Think in terms of "Am I making the absolute best impression possible?" If you don't show that you really care about yourself why would anyone else want to care?**

there's a button missing or a crooked hem, fix it. If something needs ironing, get it ironed. You may not care, but others will. Your shoes should always be polished, your nails always perfectly clean, your hat always brushed. Think in terms of: "Am I making the absolute best impression possible?" If you don't show that you really care about yourself why would anyone else want to care? This advice is for both guys and girls.

It may help to imagine you are your own public relations agent—you are the product and you want the right person not to be dissuaded from going out with you because your shoes are scruffy, your nails are dirty, your hat has a year's collection of dust, or because dandruff litters your shoulders!

However, remember that regardless of what you are wearing, it's your inside that really counts; and all the clothing in the world cannot make up for an empty inside. If you are using clothing as a means with which to feel good about yourself— sorry—but it'll never work. Although crucial, clothing, shoes, jewelry, etc. are merely external trappings and regardless of how many layers you put on—if you are missing something on the inside or are feeling insecure about yourself, it will be like putting a band aid on a broken leg—in essence these things will all be meaningless.

However, as much as we do not like the fact, we need to be physically attractive, in addition to our inner desire to be an all around "terrific person." By a "terrific person" I mean someone who will earn the respect of others and do things that are truly good.

It is that balance between our physical need to be attractive and our inner yearning to be appreciated for something deeper that makes us so unique and so human. All the elegant clothing in the world will only satisfy one part of us and leave the other side thirsty and crying for attention. As you glance through this section, remember that you are only looking at one dimension of the whole you.

Some Tried and True Clothing Tips

1. Stick to clothes you know look good. A date is a time to stick to the tried and successfully tested dating outfit, the one that encourages people to say, "Wow you look like you lost 10 pounds," or "You look great this evening." Take out and wear the clothing you know have worked before and definitely look good on you.

2. Don't wear anything too attention-getting. Remember, you want the guy to ask *you*—and not your *outfit*—out on a second date so restrain your impulse to wear a dress with big ostrich feathers flying out of it or your new hot pink neon boots. Don't wear something so flashy or gaudy that it takes the focus away from *you*.

3. Clothing expresses who you are. There is no "right way." You may decide to adopt some of our ideas, but it is really important that you take time and explore what clothing you like and what looks good on you. Clothing reveals a great deal about "you" as a person, and your style in your clothing choices reflects a very important part of who you are.

4. Neatness is everything! Whatever you wear, make sure that your clothing looks neat. Clean clothing that is neatly ironed makes a better impression than a new linen suit that crumples up every time you sit down. And on that note, make sure you wear clothing that feels comfortable. Something that untucks every time you stand up and pinches your stomach in every time you sit down will make you exceedingly self-conscious on the date.

5. Consider your date's height. Finally, figure your date into the clothing equation. Find out about height before. If he is just skimming five-feet this is not the time to drag out those four-inch stilettos. I have a friend who purchased three pairs of nearly identical black shoes all with differing heel lengths—the one-inch heels, two-inch heels and three-inch heels. Before a date, she always makes sure to ask the shadchan the guy's height, so she won't have to go prancing around the entire evening feeling like an undainty six-foot giant.

To find what you like, take a look around you. What do you like about the way other guys or girls dress? What works for others? Imitation is the best form of flattery. Ask others where they bought their clothing.

INTERVIEW WITH A SHADCHAN

Now that you have done some serious soul-searching, have written your list of desirable attributes and have bought or prepared your shidduch wardrobe, you are ready to get a date.

I enlisted the help of Rochelle Markowitz, a prominent shadchan in the Orthodox community of New York City who has been making shidduchim for more than twenty years. She generously gave of her time and agreed to do this interview.

What makes you a good shadchan?

I feel that I read people well. I'm what you call a people person. In addition, I go to more simchas and other events than does your typical single person. This helps me form connections with many people and get ideas about who to set up with whom. Single people are always busy, whether it is in school or work. I travel a great deal. This gives me the chance to meet people that a single person might never get to meet.

> I feel that it is everyone's responsibility to set up as many girls and boys as possible.

As far as setting people up, it's natural to me. How could I not do it? It's part of who I am.

You meet a single person, you imagine them with someone else you've met, how could you not pair them up together? It's such a thrill! When it works out and these two people are happy together, the excitement is incomparable!

I feel that it is everyone's responsibility to set up as many girls and boys as possible—you just have to do it. There is so much assimilation going on today in this world. I have frum girls calling me and crying that if I don't set them up with some-one, they're going to go out with someone at work who isn't frum! They say they've just had enough! I lose sleep over it. There are just so many girls in their late 20's and 30's and nobody wants to take the time out to help them.

You asked what makes me a good shadchan. I feel it is that I take the time to really listen when single people talk to me. And when I say I'm going to do something I keep to my word. I also have a great deal of patience. A shadchan has to have a lot of patience.

If I mention a girl to a guy and he takes his time getting back to me—I don't get discouraged and lose interest—I stick with it and am persistent. I take the time to listen and am committed to following through—otherwise it's not going to work. I'm devoted to being a shadchan. It's something I do every day. It's impossible for someone to say I'm going to do it one day a week or once a month. You have to make it a full-time or at least a part-time job. And the more practice you have at it, the better you get.

How many shidduchim have you made?

I've made a lot of shidduchim. As a matter of fact, I even have a baby named after me! The couple asked me what my fee was. I told them, "I don't charge a fee. I do it for the mitzvah." The boy was a rabbi and a teacher and his wife worked in a doctor's office. I made their shidduch a few years back and, *B"H*, they now have four children. They wanted to thank me in some way for helping them find each other and so they named their daughter after me—that was their gift to me.

I enjoy being a shadchan. I am, *B"H*, very happy in my marriage and I want everyone else to be happy as well. I want everybody to find their soul mate. I see so many beautiful marriages out there and I think everyone deserves to have that sort of happiness. I don't let things get me down. I believe there's a shidduch for everyone, a lid for every pot, and I'm out there always looking. If I don't find someone today, I may have someone a year down the road. The people I've agreed to match up are always on my mind.

People complain that shadchanim either don't have time for them or don't understand them. What do you feel can be done to improve this situation?

If the shadchan is consistently not nice, there's no reason to stick with him or her. There are people out there whose character it is to brush people off or to be lax about other's feelings. Don't blame yourself if a shadchan consistently disregards you. It is *not* a reflection on you. Just move on. Find a shadchan who is considerate of your feelings and takes the time to hear you out.

Just like anybody else, a shadchan might have off days. If they sound busy, try them again, but if they brush you off two or three times, *try someone else*. There are shadchanim who have chips on their shoulders because they realize how in demand they are. As a result they are callous towards the people who call them. These shadchanim should choose a different profession!

But as a single person, it's important to always be considerate. You must understand that a shadchan may have their list of priority people—such as their own family members and close friends—that he or she is obligated to work on first. I, for example, have a single niece and she is now, understandably, at the top of my priority list. A shadchan might cut you short when you call, not because she doesn't want to help you, but because she is simply overwhelmed at that particular time. In that case, be persistent! Call back in a month or two when things may have quieted down for her.

Many people say they have tried a professional shadchan once or twice but they were set up with people so completely wrong for them they wondered if the shadchan had taken the time to notice who they were and what their particular needs were.

It is possible that the shadchan didn't take time to learn about someone. A professional shadchan invests time to find out about each person individually and to discover what makes them tick. Any time a name is mentioned to me, whether it's a girl or a boy, I inquire about the individual. I call a few people and try to learn as much as I can about their character before I set them up. I'll call their rabbi or family friend to get a better picture of the person I'm dealing with. It is impossible to gain the full flavor and depth of a person after one phone conversation or even after meeting them once in person. Therefore I try to speak to many people who know this individual in a variety of situations to get a broader, more complete idea of what this person is all about. Once this is all done, I think of someone I know who would be a good match for this person. I mention the name and then tell the girl or boy that they have to check out the person I am recommending on their own. It's not like slapping two pieces of wood together randomly. You have to take the time to be meticulous and thorough and give each suggestion you make careful consideration first.

I have also found it is helpful to talk to people I am matching up two or three times over the course of our relationship to establish a closeness and friendship. This way some of the intimidation of the encounter is dissipated and they take me into their confidence. It also helps me do a better job for them. I'm not here to give a guy a phone number the second he calls. I take my time with it; I take the time to study if a boy and girl would be compatible. That's why I tell people who call me, "I may have something for you today, but if not be patient. You'll hear from me in a month or two." Setting two people up takes careful thought and I like to do it right.

Do you believe that certain people are easier than others to marry off?

Yes. Certain individuals really want to be married, which makes my job easier. Everything is timing. If you are being set up with people one after another and you have a too specific idea of what you are looking for, you'll end up rejecting people right and left because they have a dimple in the wrong place, or their nose is turned the wrong way. This kind of attitude will make it much harder for a single person. I hesitate to use the word, "settling," but in the right time when you are truly ready to get married, these things aren't going to be considered so important to you.

There are shadchanim who charge $180 for an initial appointment, $100 for every date they come up with after that, and anywhere from $2,000 to $5,000 when they make

your shidduch. How do you feel about charging money for your services?

As I said before, I don't charge. However, in no way do I look down on the shadchanim who do charge. Nobody works for nothing today! Would you take a 9 to 5 job and not get paid for it? Never! And then what about a shadchan's expenses: money spent on computers, phone bills—after all, we serve people internationally. We call all over the world to do our job well. Our phone bills are tremendous. The fee a shadchan charges covers their expenses—they are not becoming rich from this.

A shadchan makes one or two shidduchim a year, out of perhaps hundreds of people. Some have three or four shidduchim but they are the exceptions. So, they may charge $1,800 to the girl and $1,800 to the boy. If you add up their incomes, it doesn't even come close to the average 9 to 5 job. They are doing a vital mitzvah at minimum wage!

Even the shadchanim who charge $10,000 per shidduch, are likely only making a few shidduchim a year. This is their livelihood and I can't be the one to judge them. I recommend that everyone should get involved in the process of setting up people and then they'll see how difficult it is! Everyone who is reading this interview should think of two people they know who would be a good shidduch and set them up with each other. Your job is to get two of them to go out on one date. You will soon see that the amount of calling, convincing, discussing, persuading, arbitrating, and mediating you must do simply to get two people to go out on one date is so work-intensive (never mind that a shadchan must continue this calling back and forth continually throughout the dating process) that the money they receive is only a small token of appreciation!

Can you give me three reasons why you think that most shadchanim choose this work?

I do it because I find it extremely rewarding. As I mentioned, I have always been a people-person. I like helping people, so setting people up came naturally to me. Besides which, my grandfather, as well as my aunt (who made sixteen shidduchim) were both shadchanim, so it's very much in my essence to do this. It's in my blood. I grew up hearing my grandfather make shidduchim, and every time he made one I saw how excited he was. He would call up the whole family and let us all know. I saw how rewarding it was for him, as it is for me. I imagine there is no greater high than showing people their bashert and contributing to their simchah.

And finally, there is the excitement of seeing the fruits of your labor. You get to see marriages that with Hashem's help work out successfully. Then you get to see the children growing up and you can be proud of yourself that you helped bring this about.

How could a single person help a shadchan help them?

By calling them regularly, approximately every two to three

weeks is perfect. You should make a short courtesy call just to say "Hi, it's Naomi, I just wanted to remind you that I'm out there, and to find out if you have come up with anyone for me." Don't jump on them and be rude to them, by saying "What's going on? I haven't heard from you in four months.

> If you call often, a shadchan is more likely to remember you and keep you in the forefront of their mind.

How come you don't have anything for me?" I have people who call me, and as soon as I pick up the phone they are already jumping down my throat, "How come you set up that one, and she's engaged, and you never come up with anyone for my daughter and so on and so forth?" Who wants to talk to someone like that? One woman who calls me is so refreshing to speak to. She calls up and always starts with a "Hi, how are you?" Then she'll ask about me and how my life is doing. She is interested in me too, and not only with what I can be doing for her!

It's true that the squeaky kettle gets the grease. If you call often, a shadchan is more likely to remember you and keep you in the forefront of their mind. However, when you do call, remember: You will get much farther being polite and nice than acting aggressive and confrontational. And another thing, don't be shy or embarrassed to remind shadchanim that you are out there. Often we are simultaneously dealing with many people and we need a reminder. It is worth swallowing your pride and making the call. Believe me, the last thing that crosses a shadchan's mind when you call is how needy you may feel, and therefore how embarrassed you are, to be constantly reminding us of your existence. If shadchanim don't consider you to be "needy" or a "nudge" than why should you look at yourself in this way?

What would you recommend that a single girl or boy do to enhance themselves in order to get dates?

Well, for girls especially, it is important to be "put together" whenever you go out. Don't just save new outfits for special occasions. You should think of every day as a special occasion and *always* look your best. Make sure your clothes are updated. And keep in mind, you don't have to invest loads of money into looking your best. Simply keeping your clothes clean and ironed, and asking a friend or family member for an honest opinion about your wardrobe can go a long way.

Nowadays there are even professional shoppers who will take you shopping and help you choose colors which complement your complexion and styles which are the most flattering for you. If you don't want to invest in a day with a shopper, ask if you could tag-a-long one day when someone you know who has excellent taste goes shopping. Then allow them to pick out a few new pieces for you.

There are also makeup artists you can turn to if you want to go for a fresh, new look. Try getting a new haircut or wearing your hair a different way and listen to people's reactions when they see it. You do not have to look like you stepped out of Vogue magazine, but make sure you wear light, flattering makeup, and look presentable *wherever* you go.

In addition, many guys complain to me that girls aren't aware of what is going on in the world and never pick up a newspaper to find out. You can become a much more interest-

> You should do whatever you can to improve yourself, whether it means attending classes, reading, or going to lectures.

ing person to be around and a better conversationalist if you have wide, varied interests and you know about current events. Girls should pick up a newspaper every now and then to find out what's going on! Girls should also develop new likings and hobbies. Go to an occasional Jewish play or concert. When you are excited about something, it shines right through when you talk about it, and your date will admire your enthusiasm.

Read a paper or go to a shiur so you will have more to talk about on your dates. You should do whatever you can to improve yourself, whether it means attending classes, reading, or going to lectures. Going to the Himalayas for three months to find yourself is probably not a good idea, but short of that, anything you can do to better yourself and make yourself a more interesting person to be around, is a good idea. It is also important at this time to try not to be too sensitive. If someone gives you well-meaning constructive criticism, take it. And thank them for trying to help, instead of feeling insulted.

Girls and boys—don't be so sensitive when you are dating! I think of dating like making a sale. When you are going on a date you are selling yourself. What would a salesperson do if he or she wanted to make a sale? He or she would:

1. Dress well.

2. Be daring.

3. Be persistent.

4. Not fall apart if he or she gets a "no."

If a guy or girl says "no" to you after a date, shrug it off and go on. This is the most important message I can give to you—this is not the time to start taking everything personally and falling apart every time someone says no to you. Just assure yourself that the person was not worth getting upset over and you will find someone much better suited to you further on down the road.

Many people would never consider going to a shadchan and claim they would never do so. This makes many people who do, feel terrible. What's your opinion? Is there a qualitative difference between those who seek the help of a shadchan and those who don't?

The first thing I would tell you is—don't always believe the people who say they would never go to a shadchan. Two weeks ago a girl called me up. She asked me if I knew someone for her and for her brother, both of whom were looking to get married. I looked through my file and I came up with someone for her, and then I thought of someone who would be perfect for her brother. When I mentioned the girl's name to her, she exclaimed, "You must be kidding, she just told me how pathetic I was for going to see a shadchan. 'What do you need a shad-chan for?' she asked me. "And here she is, registered with you!"

Many girls feel insecure and self-conscious about enlisting a shadchan's help. The truth of the matter is, the majority of them do it and there is nothing to feel embarrassed about. There is no qualitative difference between those who seek a shadchan's help and those who don't. It is just the concept of getting "help" that some people have trouble with. Instead they should realize one can get much farther in life when one takes advice and guidance from others and learns from other's mistakes. In life, you have to fight your own battles and be your own cheering squad. Whatever you need to do to get where you want to in life—within the confines of halachah—should be done.

Can you leave single people with any final words of encouragement?

I would say to everyone—your shidduch will come! You just have to have patience. And one more thing, don't run away from it. I find some people I set up are so entangled in their careers and their traveling and fun, that they almost seem to be running away from marriage. You can have a satisfying career and travel and have fun when you are married! If you are deter-mined enough you can make the time for everything, so give yourself that shove and make marriage your #1 priority.

Action Steps

1. Call your shadchan regularly.

2. Be polite when you speak to your shadchan and take an interest in their lives.

3. Do whatever you can to enhance yourself (look your best, develop varied interests) and make yourself a better date.

4. If a guy or girl says no, shrug it off and go on.

5. Chin up and relax, your shidduch will come!

HOW TO FIND A GOOD DATE (AND I DON'T MEAN THE FRUIT)

Now that you've heard the scoop from a shadchan, you may or may not decide to call one. Here I will detail where else you can find good candidates to date. Just finding the right person to date will take some work on your part. But once you have given a great deal of thought to it and have truly decided that you are ready to get married, you will have to focus your complete attention on finding yourself the most perfect date—someone whose background is appropriate and whose values match yours.

If you'd like, you can think of it as a battle to win (a.k.a. MISSION: DATE) and nothing short of a nuclear blow-out will stand in your way. It's like taking on a new career—you'll need to focus and spend time every day working and net-working trying to find a serious candidate for marriage.

WHERE TO LOOK FOR A DATE

The first place to look in your quest for a date is:

Your Neighborhood Shadchan

Many people have accumulated a long list of shadchanim and called them all, only to discover that the shadchanim seemed as excited talking to them as they would talking to an intestinal parasite. The shadchan simply didn't seem to feel their case was important and ended the phone conversation with a non-committal, "We'll see what we can do."

Here are some typical reasons your shadchan may give you as to why they can't set you up. I have included a possible response on your part, followed by a correct, more appropriate response that will hopefully push you higher up on their priority list. And, by the way, the shadchan I refer to here could be a friend, relative or a community member—anyone who has the wherewithal to set you up with some quality individuals.

Shadchan's Reasons Why They Can't Set You Up:

1. *I know some nice guys or girls but none of them are good enough for you.*

Wrong response: Oh really, I'm not as great as you think.

Correct response: I think I'd like to give them a chance and decide for myself if they are right for me. Tell me more about them. Maybe there's a possibility it could work.

2. *If I set you up with someone and it doesn't work out it* *could ruin our friendship.*

Wrong response: Who needs friends, I need a husband (or a wife)!

Correct response: Oh, please don't worry! I would never hold it against you if the date didn't work out. I would just appreciate it when you set me up. I understand that it's not always going to be a perfect fit. If the guy/girl is not for me our friendship would always continue. (I should add here that when you are set up with someone who is all wrong for you, you might feel angry, blow up or hold a grudge, thinking, "What does this person think of me?" However, please keep in mind that we are all mere mortals. Only G-d has the vision to know which two people will ultimately "go" with one another. Be understanding when you are set up! Make an effort to appreciate the tiresome work involved in bringing two people together—even if the guys/girls they set you up with are totally off base. Your friends are not trying to be malicious or mean by setting you up with the, "Where'd-she-get-this-one-from?" type of girl or guy. If your friends are taking the time and effort necessary to set you up, then you can be sure that they have your best interest at heart and are trying their best.)

3. *I don't know anyone for you.*

Wrong response: You're not trying hard enough. You must know somebody!

Correct response: I just wanted to let you know, I really appreciate everything you've been doing for me up until now. (Or if it's the first time you're calling—I really wanted to thank you for doing this for me.) And please keep your eyes and ears open. If G-d happens to drop someone down that you think would be good for me, please send him or her my way!

Good Dates Are All Around You

Apart from people who officially establish themselves as a "shadchan," you can call on plenty of regular people—people you meet at the kosher takeout, people waiting next to you at the barber or hairdresser, and all the people you've been connected with in some way during the past ten years. The truly

> The truly successful people in this world are those who can call on others to help them.

successful people in this world are those who can call on others to help them. We cannot attend every kiddush, be seen at every wedding, and consult with every shadchan ourselves! We need to mobilize the right people to help us.

Make a point about once a month to pull out your phone book and let your fingers do the walking. Start with A and end at Z and reconnect with old friends and acquaintances. Call them and, sounding as natural as possible, ask them about their lives, their family, children, job, and favorite projects. Once you've established yourself as someone who cares and is interested in their life, you can drop your sales pitch. Add a line simply saying, "By the way, I am dating now, do you happen to know anyone for me?" This way they are much more likely to think of you next time somebody asks them if they know someone for their niece or nephew.

Some people, understandably, will feel uneasy calling people they haven't spoken to in years and reconnecting with them. However, just think how happy you are when an old friend you haven't spoken to in years calls you to catch up on old times. Most people enjoy being filled in on the lives of those they care about and will be thrilled to hear from you!

Once you've started reconnecting with old friends, buy a small notebook to keep by the phone and label it, "shidduchim prospects." Whenever somebody mentions a name for you, jot it down. Next to it, write the basic information such as: age, yeshiva, job, goals, personality, references, and most importantly—who is willing to set the date up—with their phone number. The following week or so check into the person you were set up with and find out if they are what you are looking for in a life partner. Then you can call back the person who set you up. You cannot imagine how many great shidduchim have never happened because of the failure to get back to people who have casually mentioned a possible match.

The best way I have found to keep on top of one's shidduch life is to keep a dating-tab in your notebook. Every mentioned prospect should have a month and day next to his or her name informing you when you first heard their name. After that, whenever you call the person who set you up, you could jot down all the information in your book next to the date of when you first heard the name. Wait a week from the time you let the shadchan know you are interested until you call again to find out his or her answer. Be persistent and time-conscious and don't let those casual suggestions slip by you.

Being Nice To Everybody Can Get You Good Dates

It's no joke, the guy selling the kishka at the kosher take-out might really know someone for you. You want to make a point of being as friendly as possible to everyone you meet and not turning away any possible date suggesters.

A friend of mine taught preschool in a local yeshiva, and one day a boy in her class (a whopping four-year-old!) asked her, "Do you want to get married? Because if you do I have an uncle that's not married." She laughed the child off and chalked it up to an overactive imagination. Two days later he brought in a picture of his uncle to show to her and he asked her, "Do you want to date him?" In the end, the two didn't go for each other. (Nowadays, she laughingly says—if it would have worked, what would have been shadchan gelt? A Power Ranger?) You never know who will be the *shaliach* to bring you your shidduch. So it pays to smile at everyone and take an extra minute to say something nice.

Become Like The Person You'd Like To Date

Most of us are looking for a marriage partner with certain characteristics. Thus it makes sense to incorporate some of those qualities within ourselves. So, for instance, if you are looking for someone who is good-hearted, compassionate, generous and enthusiastic about life, make sure you assimilate these characteristics into your own character. If you are looking to support someone in kollel and intend to have a home devoted to chesed, it makes sense to help out at the local chesed and gemach organizations thus identifying yourself as someone who values this sort of lifestyle. This serves a few purposes. You will find out if this is really who you are and really what you want. People around you will then be quick to ascertain what your needs are in a marriage partner based on the life you have carved out for yourself. Plus your involvement in chesed and gemach organizations will put you in touch with other compassionate people, and they will then become another possible source for dates.

Action Steps

1. Ask people you know to help you find a shadchan.

2. Once you have a list of shadchanim, call them and describe yourself and what kind of person you're looking for.

3. Call all the people you know and let them know you're ready to get married. Ask them to keep you in mind for anyone they think would be suitable.

4. Realize that anyone around you could lead you to your bashert. Be the best you can be all the time!

5. Continue developing your personality—become more like the person you'd like to find!

MARS AND VENUS
ON A SHIDDUCH DATE

It is not farfetched or presumptuous to say that men and women are so different in their approach to shidduchim that they can be considered to be from two different cultures, and, yes, even from two different planets, and when they get together, it can be considered a cross-cultural or even interplanetary experience.

When a frum boy is young, extra effort, money and time is expended on the part of his parents to make sure that he can recite a piece of gemarah at the Shabbos table, learn the parshah and its commentaries, and take his overall Torah studies seriously.

At a young age boys are commended when they can answer the rebbe's question or better yet—can come up with a question that even their rebbe can't answer. Their school day can end as late as 9:00 p.m., as well as having a full day on Sunday, and there is little time after that to develop their personal interests. "*Bitul zeman*" or wasting time is shunned.

In addition to a boy's Torah pursuits, many parents encourage their sons to start planning for a future career so that one day they can become a good provider. Between these two pursuits, most boys have little time left for anything else.

> **Men and women are so different in their approach to shidduchim that when they get together, it can be considered a cross-cultural —or even interplanetary— experience.**

While a girl is definitely encouraged to learn the Torah laws and philosophies necessary to run a future household and fine-tune her middos to become a good wife and mother, such in-depth Torah study is not demanded.

Bitul zeman is not an issue with girls—most of whom are home from school at 5:00 p.m. Yes, they are given loads of homework, but most have a chance to take piano lessons, indulge in an Israeli dance class, and talk on the phone to their friends till the wee hours of the night. Girls cultivate the simple pleasures of connecting intimately with friends and develop the verbal and interpersonal skills that will help them throughout their life. Girls also cultivate their ability to be compassionate, understanding, or just be there to hear someone else out, or help others in volunteer chesed activities.

While boys connect with each other and communicate via their learning (i.e. the *chavrusah* system), girls do not use their learning as a reference point for communication. Two girls can spend an afternoon over lunch sharing their feelings, secrets, needs and desires. Boys' communication is usually more specific and linked to talmudic studies, a historic or current event or some concrete thing—like fixing a car.

A mother encourages her daughter to be a good listener, to be caring, kind and attentive to other people's needs and to always look her best. A father encourages his son to be Torah knowledgeable, to earn a *parnassah*, be self-confident, responsible and an all-around mentch.

When a boy and a girl from two essentially different cultures and two different types of exposure meet on a shidduch date, the results can be quite interesting. The two have been brought up in almost completely separate worlds and have rarely even talked to the opposite gender. This transition from limited communication with the opposite gender to open and free conversation is often difficult for both the girl and the boy to adjust to.

But, before you run away and say, "It's hopeless, I'll never understand *them*," (and *both* girls and boys say this!) read this chapter carefully. If you are better informed about how the world of guys operates, or how the world of girls operates, you might be able to avoid some of the obstacles along the road.

I must give a special thanks at this point to my parents and mentors for helping me write this chapter. If, when reading it, you find yourself saying, "This is a generalization and plainly doesn't apply to me"—that is perfectly okay. As with all other things in life, there are often many exceptions to the rule. A few of the points mentioned below have been adapted from John Gray's best-selling book, *Men are from Mars, Women are From Venus*.

A girl and a boy meet. She's accustomed to free association in her communication with her friends and he's accustomed to speaking in a more concrete manner. How do they bridge the gap?

A girl arrives at the dating setting after years of fine tuning her communication skills. Whether it's on the phone with friends or over tea, she has perfected the skill of just chatting. She uses speech as a tool to connect with the people around her. When one of her friends is down she will call her or drive right over to her house with a card and just listen to her friend pour out her feelings and she will offer her friend solace and advice. She will attempt to be understanding and compassionate and demonstrate to her friend how concerned she is about her well being.

Two guys chatting are most likely to talk of more solid concrete things like education, cars, business ideas or sports events and feelings will be prominently left out of it. And although they will be concerned when their friend is down, they will actually prefer to leave him alone rather than dig too deeply into the matter.

One way for the two genders to bridge the gap is to

acknowledge these differences and adapt to them—a girl can use her talent at communication to brighten up the more technical aspects of a guy's conversation. He in turn can use his factual knowledge to balance her free association. The key here is that each of them, using their particular well-honed communication skills, can add more interest and balance to the conversation.

A man is generally looking for someone who will validate him and make him feel respectable. He searches for someone who is easy to please and shows an interest in him. A woman is looking for an anchor, someone she can rely on. She especially is happy when a man takes the time to ask about her hobbies and her work and seems genuinely interested in knowing about her.

A guy and a girl will bridge the gap by complementing each other's needs and caring enough to provide these needs for the other person. Show your appreciation when a guy brings flowers on a date, chooses a nice restaurant to take you to, opens the door for you or makes a special effort to be nice to your parents, by simply saying, "Thanks—I really appreciate what you've done." Remember, a man thrives on being appreciated for his efforts.

On the other hand, a girl is looking for someone who'll pay attention to her, asking her how she feels and what she is thinking and then taking the time to *really* listen. A girl wants to hear that a guy will think of her, be interested in her needs and what she does during the day, and will be someone she can rely on.

A man is often looking for someone who will create a harmonious home for him, a place where he can feel comfortable bringing home his learning, and filling the environment with kedushah. A woman is searching for a man who will bring the kedushah into the home.

A guy often is looking for a woman who will ensure a home of tranquility, harmony and peace, a place to which he will look forward to coming home to at night. A guy wants a place where his Torah knowledge as well as his business acumen will be valued. He wants a place with a relaxing, stress-free atmosphere where he can come for recharging to face to rigors of the day ahead, whether it is in Torah learning or in professional endeavors or both.

A girl, on the other hand, usually look for a guy who will take his Yiddishkeit seriously. In school she is taught to look for a guy who is one rung higher than she on the "spiritual ladder." "Always look for someone who is one step up"—she is told. She is generally looking for someone who, even if not immersed in the Torah world full time as a rebbe or learner and is working (which is totally fine!), is a ben Torah and values a Torah way of life.

She is looking for certain qualities in a guy, namely, someone who is kind, flexible, understanding, and committed to her happiness. He in turn is looking for an *"ezer kinegdo,"* someone who will nurture him, comfort him when he's down, be excited for him when things are going well, encourage him at all times, and give him the strength to pursue his Torah and career goals.

A guy usually comes to a date while he is in or shortly after he has left the yeshivah world. He is usually coming from a more insular environment where he is surrounded by people similar to him. Girls' experiences, on the other hand, are usually more disparate.

A girl, after a year of seminary (if she attended one) will find herself in college, the work force, or both, being exposed to a diverse array of people and situations. She will become accustomed to working and talking with people from all walks of life. Entering the work force in any capacity (yes, even for a Jewish company), will make her more savvy in the ways of the world.

With G-d's help, she has a firm enough Torah foundation to withstand its influences. She acknowledges the worth of her heritage and she values above all her family and her Torah values. Her Torah way of life is her steady guide and with little difficulty she can compartmentalize her time in college and work and not let it spill over into the other areas of her life. A guy who understands this, has a real edge in understanding and appreciating what a girl is about. And a girl who remembers that many guys are less experienced with the world at large will be more understanding.

While a guy often searches for a girl who is intelligent and bright he will usually not want someone who will show him up or compete with him. A girl will honestly admit that she wants and needs someone at least as clever as her in Torah ways as well as general smarts.

When a guy is giving a d'var Torah in front of a girl's father, one of the worst things a girl can do is contradict him or not pay attention. Men are highly sensitive about their knowledge and it would not be a girl's place to correct him right there. This poses somewhat of a problem for some girls who have attended rigorous seminaries and have a vast storehouse of Torah knowledge to draw on. It would be important to learn when it's appropriate to share their Torah knowledge and when to make a guy feel like a guy and avoid interrupting or contradicting him. Certainly when a guy is involved in a Torah discussion or any other discussion for that matter, she should feel free to enter her input and add to the conversation.

Most guys will love to hear a girl's opinion and will even enjoy a friendly argument with her if she does not share his views. However, just as a girl would not appreciate being told, "That's not right, I learned it differently," a guy who has invested so much time and effort into his Torah learning would find this extremely hurtful.

A girl is exceedingly interested in the relationship and how it is working out. Girls spend time analyzing what went

on and make a bigger deal about the little details—i.e., he didn't notice my new haircut, sweater, shoes; he didn't open the door for me; he didn't say he had a great time after the date; he didn't call me the next night; and the ten possible messages each of these things was supposed to send.

While a girl analyzes everything in terms of what it means to the relationship, if things are generally going well, a guy is more likely to go along with it and not examine the little details of conversation. Guys do not generally break down the relationship into tiny, minuscule parts. Instead, they look at the overall picture and see what's happening. Knowing how important little details are to a girl you are dating, a guy should put in that extra effort to notice, compliment, take note of the small things.

A girl works so hard at making sure she looks just so— from her nails down to her coordinating scarf, and will always appreciate a fine compliment. A girl in turn can give the guy confidence that the relationship is going well by making the big things count. Remarks such as, "You seem like a great learner," or "I could tell you invest a great deal of effort into your work," or "This was a great evening—I had a great time," or "I really enjoy your divrei Torah," or "Your car is so clean," go a long way.

Girls are generally better at communicating their feelings. They tend to be more open about how they are feeling and are quicker to share how they feel.

It is simply *not* a guy thing to sit around a yeshivah or college dorm and say, "I am having really positive feelings about going to visit so and so this Sunday." Nor are you likely to hear one of them say, "I feel Dovid is jealous of me because I am doing better in the class/I got a new car etc." This, however, is typical girl conversation.

While opening up about feelings may be more difficult for some guys, and many girls do instinctively know that guys will clam up in this area, an understanding that occasionally a girl just wants and needs to hear how a guy feels in a certain situation, will really make a girl happy. Realize that although it's frightening for many guys to reveal their feelings it really shows a girl you care.

The roles of a guy and a girl when shidduch dating arises from two very different angles.

A girl is usually the one who does the most waiting. One thing shidduchim can do for a girl is build patience. She will wait for a shadchan to call or wait for a certain shidduch to materialize. The *last* thing she wants to do is appear desperate and needy. The guy, on the other hand, tends to have a more active role in the shidduch process. Between calling the girl, planning the date, and letting the shadchan know if he's interested, he definitely appears to be taking a more pro-active position.

There are two parts to this issue, however. Girls are often frustrated before an actual date and even on the date itself. Before a date, girls often feel that it is out of their hands and they just have to wait for something/someone to materialize. If you feel this way you should remember that you do not have to be passive in this area. By calling shadchanim, previous teachers, married friends and just talking or taking Shabbos invitations to these people's houses, you will be remembered

> A girl enjoys being "taken out" and made to feel as if the guy did some thinking and planning before he showed up at her door.

in these people's minds. Even calling up an old acquaintance from shul or high school and saying, "I think we could help each other when it comes to shidduchim in terms of setting each other up" would be a good idea.

On the actual date itself, most girls will appreciate it if the guy drives, opens the door for her and plans something special (i.e. gets tickets to a ball game, makes reservations to a nice restaurant—in short takes the active role in making sure the date runs smoothly). A girl enjoys being "taken out" and made to feel as if the guy did some thinking and planning before he showed up at her door.

Finally, there is a Torah commentary that explains that Adam and Chavah were initially created as one. G-d later split them to make them two unique entities who would eventually unite once again and become husband and wife. It is for this reason that some commentaries explain that making shidduchim is as difficult as splitting the Red Sea—because Adam and Chavah were literally "split" down the center and were later united again in marriage.

Even though a guy and a girl may at times seem to be coming from different worlds—just as Adam and Chavah were created as one and then split—so, too, the neshamos of a boy and a girl who are destined to be married were initially joined, then split when they entered the world, only to be one day reunited. They spend the first part of their life searching for their other half to be a "whole" once again.

So while men and woman at times seem to be completely different, their job is to complement each other, balancing each other's different personality traits, and becoming a more complete whole.

A woman and man might understand things in a different light, but it takes each of their individual lights brought together to brighten the world!

Action Steps

If you just figured out that guys and girls are different—you are right! Knowing this is a great first step toward understanding each other, respecting each other and learning to get along....

HISHTADLUS (PERSONAL EFFORT) VS. BITACHON (TRUSTING IN G-D) WHEN DATING

Leah takes dating seriously. Since she entered the twelfth grade she has never been seen in an outfit costing less than $150. Her hair is always perfect, her manners unfailingly charming, regardless of her mood or to whom she is talking. She is in shul almost every single Shabbos and Yom Tov, and does not leave until she has greeted almost every woman individually.

Leah goes to all sorts of lengths to "pursue" shiduchim. She has had to swallow her pride on several occasions when it came to calling strangers about a boy she has seen or heard about who might be even a remote possibility for her. She makes sure her name is at the top of every prospective shadchan's list, and devotes a substantial amount of time and effort to this pursuit.

Leah will never allow herself to "dump" a boy she has been set up with, no matter how she actually feels about him. By being the one to terminate the relationship, she fears that she will place herself in the unenviable position of "losing her bashert." Leah feels that by pushing every relationship to the limit, she is showing Hashem her *hishtadlus* and eagerness.

Rachel, Leah's best friend, thinks Leah has gone off the deep end. Nearly all of Rachel's outfits are bargain-priced, as she prefers to save her money for future needs. She only attends shul when she feels like it, and only speaks to people to whom she has something to say.

Unlike Leah, Rachel allows her pride to prevent her from pursuing shidduchim. Also, she will not contact a shadchan if she has had a bad experience with him or her. Rachel never, ever goes out a second time with a guy whom she does not like—no matter how superficial her reason might seem to others.

In reading the above vignettes, one might come to the conclusion that Leah will surely get married first. Leah is certainly making every imaginable effort to increase her odds, while Rachel is, if anything, cutting off possibilities. However, while Leah may be winning the *hishtadlus* contest, *hishtadlus* alone will unfortunately *not* get anybody married—and I think this point is something we sometimes forget. We think we can do it all, and with just the right bit of this and that, we can maneuver our lives just the way we would like them to be. No one, no matter what lengths they will go to, will find their bashert until G-d has deemed it the appropriate time.

Does this mean that one should throw one's hands up (as Rachel seems to be doing) and not make any effort? Surely not—our Rabbis teach that a combination of *hishtadlus* and *bitachon is* necessary to achieve every goal. However, many people who are dating tend to err by leaning toward one or the other extreme (often encouraged by their parents).

> **Our Rabbis teach that a combination of <u>hishtadlus</u> and <u>bitachon</u> is necessary to achieve one's every goal in life.**

Only a Rabbi can tell a dater or his or her parents when they are going too far. However, as a longtime observer of (and participant in) the Flatbush dating scene, I have found it far more common for people to err by not leaving enough up to G-d. Shidduchim affords parents the freedom to pick and choose among the details of various resumes before allowing their children to meet prospective matches. Unfortunately, this tends to give them an illusion of control which they do not actually have.

When parents can control the details of a prospective date's background, from his/her height to his/her educational level to his/her family background, they begin to feel as if they are also in control of this scary, uncontrollable, and unpredictable situation. Every new factor which they prescribe before the date perpetuates this fallacy. Seeking and screening out dates becomes almost a game as parents work furiously to determine their children's future.

In so doing, parents are actually setting up a facade which allows them to deny the significant role of mazal in this process. Years later, as their children remain single, many burnt-out parents despairingly throw up their hands and wonder where they went wrong. Was there a shadchan they failed to contact, a shidduch they failed to follow up? Have they been too picky? What they fail to realize is that, without Hashem's deciding that the time is right, their *hishtadlus*, while necessary, is not sufficient.

Some people may find this insight depressing since it reminds us how helpless we are. In fact, it should have the opposite effect. Rather than making us feel helpless, it should take some of the pressure off—we should feel affirmed in knowing that our efforts will yield fruit—if properly directed.

In *Tehillim* Dovid Hamelech says, "*Hashlech al Hashem yahavchah, veHu yechalkelecha*—Cast your burden upon Hashem and He will sustain you" (55:23). Davening, engaging in acts of chesed, and making strides to improve ourselves are efforts which can potentially affect Hashem's decision for us. While the more earthly *hishtadlus* of networking and creating a good impression everywhere has its place, we can probably do far more good if we append actions to a larger attempt to enact change on a spiritual level.

Action Steps

1. We sometimes maintain the illusion that we are in total control when in reality our lives are in Hashem's hands.

2. When seeking to create a future for yourself (or, for parents, for your child) do everything you can, but expect mazal to play a role as well.

3. Know that by improving yourself spiritually you can potentially affect Hashem's plans for you.

REASONS PEOPLE SAY NO WHEN THEY SHOULD RECONSIDER

People give many reasons why some perfectly good person was not for them. Some of the reasons are really well thought out and deeply felt. However, other reasons should be examined a little more deeply. Perhaps you'll find that it is in the logic of these reasons where your problem may lie.

1. The Guy Or Girl Was Too "Attainable"

Some people, unfortunately, feel that someone too attainable will *not* make a good candidate for marriage. They yearn for the unattainable—someone who seems interesting but who never seems to notice them, someone who is a challenge. Although this is altogether too common, it is an absolutely unhealthy attitude.

A healthy person seeks a nice, loving person who will

respect them and try their hardest to treat them well, someone who is authentically interested in their needs and dreams, someone who is not into "playing hard to get," or any other silly dating game.

However, even healthy people sometimes fall into unhealthy traps—and are attracted to the unattainable. They are attracted to guys or girls who clearly are not interested in them—it can even be as extreme as girls being interested in macho, hard-to-get guys who aren't very nice. Or guys interested in girls who act coldly toward them. Psychologists say that the reasons people tend to this are complex.

For some people this is a self-esteem issue. These people don't believe they are truly likeable. To prove this they deliberately pursue people who wouldn't want them, as if to drill it into themselves how unlikeable they really are! They'll think—if someone likes me, there must be something wrong with them. The comedian Groucho Marx once said, "I wouldn't join any club that would have me as a member"—which aptly summarizes this attitude. One woman I know once confided to me as if it were a sad unchangeable fact, "They have to reject me, and then I like them!" The more a guy doesn't want her, the more she thinks he's the man for her.

Other people view a guy or a girl saying "no" to them as a challenge. Once a girl says "no" to a guy—although he wouldn't otherwise have been interested—he transforms her into a challenge and relentlessly attempts to gain her affection. Perhaps it's a hunter's instinct that is suddenly triggered. And this chase can continue for years, during which time he plans to be in every restaurant, get invited to every wedding, and go anywhere where there is the remotest possibility of seeing this girl. He'll go through all of this just so this girl might see him and at last change her mind.

> **Chasing after the unattainable can become a habit—it may take strength to face the past and break old, bad habits—but, remember, you deserve more.**

One girl I met became immediately intrigued by a guy who said "no" to her. She wasted two years waiting for him to change his mind, during which time she arranged for many other people to suggest the shidduch to him. Fortunately, she finally found the common sense to move on and marry someone else—a nice, kind man who is truly interested in her. For two years she had pined away, throwing away her time and investing her emotions in a guy who didn't know she was alive. Instead she could have gone on with her life and moved on to other more appropriate (read: *more available*) prospects.

Psychologists say another reason people may act in this way is because this is simply an old psychological pattern—a person who is attracted to the unattainable may have had a parent whom they strived to be loved by but who remained distant. Chasing after the unattainable can become a habit—it may take strength to face the past and break old, bad habits—but, remember, you deserve more! Just repeat to yourself every moment you can—"I deserve to find someone who will care about me!" You may need to seriously work on building your self-esteem—and this may even entail going into therapy! But understand that falling for people who don't care about you is not only a dangerous habit, it will force you to waste precious time.

Some people can't explain why they continually seek out people who don't want them. They only say things like, "I don't know, it's like some sort of mental imbalance. I like what I can't have." What's astonishing is that most of the time the people they seek don't seem to have any special qualities—they can be nothing to look at, have a job in a laundromat, and be nothing much as far as middos are concerned, but for some inexplicable reason their mind is set on this individual.

You only hurt yourself when you set up these kinds of obstacles. Your goal should be to look for someone who will provide you with warmth, encouragement and signs that they like you. Learn to appreciate it when someone says, "I like spending time with you," or "I enjoy talking to you." You deserve it! The most important thing in a dating setting is to be a mentch and to treat the person you are with like a mentch as well. Ask yourself after each date, "What did I do to make her feel like a princess or him feel like a prince."

One girl I know—let's call her Rachel—often falls under the "Go out with boy. Boy says no. Suddenly she's interested" phenomenon. Her father is so fed up with her "games" that he jokingly threatens that he's going to find a guy who she likes and tell him to reject her. Her father says that it's only this way that she will ever walk down the aisle!

Chazal were really onto something when they said, *"mayim genuvim yimtaku—stolen waters are sweeter."* It is a universal truth that things we can't possess seem more desirable than that which we can possess.

One guy Rachel had gone out with was eager to set up repeated dates and took her to the finest, most elegant restaurants hoping to earn her favor.

> **Fear of marriage could be rooted in different areas. Only you can look into yourself and discover what makes you do the things you do and why you may be terrified of getting married.**

For Rachel this guy was just *too* nice. For girls like Rachel a nice guy is someone you can step on and someone for whom they can't muster any respect. They are more attracted to a guy who perhaps doesn't have good middos, doesn't always show up on time, and might even be flippant about their feelings. It is precisely this behavior that makes them a challenge—someone worthy of winning over, someone *truly* worthy of respect. They are intrigued by the chase, the hunt.

If you can identify this pattern within yourself it's not hopeless! There are tools with which you can try to help yourself break out of it.

Relationship consultant Maxine Freedman told me that fear of commitment and serious conflicts about marriage could lead to running after an unattainable pipe dream. This enables you to distract yourself without ever getting to the root of what's really keeping you from getting married. As I've outlined, fear of marriage could be rooted in different areas. Only you can look into yourself and discover what makes you do the things you do and why you may be terrified of getting married.

Identify what *your* personal obstacle is, either through your own introspective hard work or with the help of a rav or a psychologist. Hopefully, once this problem is addressed, you will find yourself attracted to more attainable individuals.

2. He's Too Nice

Another issue that I frequently hear is something labeled "the nice guy problem." Guys don't seem to have a big problem with girls who are too nice. Women, on the other hand, are attracted to power. No, I am not referring to a black belt in karate. For some, power could be a man who is well-known to be very learned; for others it could be a man who is financially successful, or a great intellect or someone who displays beautiful middos. When a woman says a guy was "too nice," she usually means that he overdid it and that he compromised some of his own integrity. He seemed to lack backbone. She might have done or said something not particularly nice but because he liked her so much, he didn't flinch or draw the line. He was lax with his own honor. If a man compromises his own honor, many women will feel that he has put himself down—and this is not something she will respect.

If you are a girl who has had this problem with someone you are dating, talk about it. Say it straight—"You compromised yourself by doing so and so, and I wished you wouldn't have." Take a risk and talk it out before you dismiss the person as lacking self-respect.

Someone with a soft, easy-going nature is sometimes mistaken as being too nice. However, a man like this will actually bring wonderful benefits to a marriage. His compassionate side means he won't be a stickler. He won't be tense if supper is not on the table the minute he comes home, and if the baby needs changing, he'll do it gladly and won't say, "That's your job!"

A too-nice guy may be shy, insecure or whatever! But if you are supportive and trusting and show a guy you have total confidence in him, you can help him develop a tremendous sense of self.

3. No Bells Went Off

People also reject suitable dates because they say "no bells went off" or "I don't feel anything." They might say, "I want to hear liberty bells, Fourth of July stuff! I want firecrackers and confetti!" When they return from a date and the date was just okay, they feel like a deflated balloon. My aunt often repeats something she heard from Rabbi Helman at Bais Yaakov High School: "If you expect sparks and you want stars, take a hammer and hit yourself over the head!"

If you expect romance—remember—as a shidduch dater you are looking for someone who would make a good life partner! "Tachlis—you're lucky if you get a soda!" Going on a shidduch date means you must focus on whether you can talk together, whether you think similarly, and if you have things in common.

A shidduch date is a serious and a complex thing. Finding a good shidduch entails discovering someone you can communicate with, someone who shares similar values, someone who you truly respect and like. The need for fireworks is dangerous because it is *not* a foundation on which to base a long-term relationship. (For more on this see page 17.)

4. Can't Tell One Date From Another

A friend received a call one Motzei Shabbos, just as she was preparing to attend a party. The girl on the phone sounded totally frantic. "There's this great guy from Los Angeles in New York for the weekend," she said. "He's good looking, an excellent learner, sweet as sugar, outgoing, fun, and has an excellent job as an investment banker. I know it's a little last minute, but one of his dates just canceled on him and he can fit you in tomorrow for the 4:00 p.m. to 6:00 p.m. slot. Say yes, or you'll regret it!" My friend waited for the girl to catch her breath and then replied, "Can I take the 1:00 p.m. to 3:00 p.m. slot, I have a date tomorrow night at 7:15 p.m."

"No. The 1:00 p.m. to 3:00 p.m. slot is already taken—he has them stacked up back to back from morning to night—but I'll be sure to let him know to bring you back on time so you'll make it for your next date."

Before my friend had any idea what she was getting herself into, she had agreed to go out with the lean-mean-dating machine from 4:00 p.m. to 6:00 p.m. the following day. She seriously wondered how she could get to know the guy in 120 minutes, or 7,200 seconds, but she decided to give it a shot anyway.

After the date, I got a call from her and she sounded a little down; the guy had said "no" to her. "How could he say no to me, he didn't even know me?" she asked me, quite befuddled. The poor guy (no names mentioned!) came to the date looking totally lost, or as she put it, "He looked like he had overdosed on dates." She was convinced he had taken the two previous girls to the same place. She reached this conclusion when they got into the place, and her date asked the guy behind the desk, "So what's the score now?" and began a lengthy discussion about the baseball game that was taking place that day as if the two of them had known each other for years.

The one thing my friend and her date had in common was that they both spent the duration of the date looking at their watches to make sure they would be back in time for their next dates:

> **Him:** *"So, do you have any hobbies?"*
> **Her:** (Look at watch—5:48 p.m.) *"Dancing and karate."*
> **Him:** *"Do you like any specific types of music?"*
> **Her:** (Look at watch—5:50 p.m.) *"I like jazz."*
> **Him:** (Look at watch—5:52 p.m.) *"I think we better go."*
> **Her:** *"Yup, I think we better."*

I imagine on the plane ride home the next day, the guy was thinking, "I'm sure I liked one of them, the only problem is I can't remember which one!"

Dating is serious! If you schedule four dates in one day, there is no way you can give any of them attention. You will more than likely mix them all up and end up having peculiar conversations:

> **Her:** *"So how do you like being an accountant?"*
> **Him:** *"I'm not an accountant! I'm a stock broker."*
> **Her:** *"Right, I'm sorry. So how did you enjoy growing up in Pittsburgh?"*
> **Him:** *"Are you sure you got the right one here? I'm from Queens, not Pittsburgh!"*

Doubling and tripling-up dates in one day will just cause you to casually cross out guys or girls for no reason except that you were too tired and confused to give them attention. Had the situation been different and had you given them your undivided attention, and invested the proper amount of time needed to get to know the person, you might have even liked one of them.

5. Zero Feelings Of Attraction

Attraction is not something that should be minimized. In fact, the Torah clearly says that a girl must see the man she is going to marry *before* she agrees to be wed to him in order to be certain that she is attracted to him.

Attraction, according to relationship consultant Maxine Freedman, means that you feel that this person is handsome or pretty. You like their personality and feel good around them. The feeling you get when you are with this person is like the pull of a magnet—there is just some inexplicable force attracting you to this individual. You've assessed the person's character and ideals and you like them.

Attraction, unlike "bells going off," is good and necessary since it is based not on euphoria or fantasy. A fantasy is about going high up in the clouds and knowing full well that when you fall the impact will be painful. It is not a sound basis for a relationship. More importantly, it is not a good

> **A relationship with the proper blend of attraction and shared values, can leave you feeling healthy and well-satisfied.**

reason to marry someone—similar goals, values and lifestyles are. Think of the differences between a gourmet meal and an ice-cream sundae with all the toppings. A good well-balanced gourmet meal, like a relationship with the proper blend of attraction and shared values, can leave you feeling healthy and well-satisfied. An ice-cream sundae, provides the same elated rush as in a relationship where bells go off; it might taste good at first but you cannot live on ice cream—you would get malnourished if you tried to. And once you've had ice cream every day for a week you'll yearn for something more substantial.

When a shidduch is unfolding, there are many things that come up that act as little hurdles which must be overcome if the shidduch is to continue. Each of these hurdles must be individually examined to ascertain what is indeed something negative that would end the dating interaction, and what can be worked at so that the two parties involved can continue seeing each other. One of those hurdles often heard when someone stops dating someone else is "I'm not attracted to him/her."

At a lecture on relationships given by Rikki Cohen, a prominent businessman and Torah scholar in the Brooklyn Syrian community, someone asked, "What if I'm just not attracted to the girl—let's say she has a wart on her face." His response, which I thought astute: "We all have warts."

"As a matter of fact," he continued, "We all have many warts, some of which are big and ugly. You should not consider it 'settling' if you take a girl or a boy who has a wart because none of us is perfect. If you look at yourself objectively, both physically and internally, you will find many things that are short of perfect."

In summary, beauty is not only skin-deep, but comes from a much deeper source. There are many physically attractive people who have undesirable qualities that once you get to know them will detract from their beauty. In turn, one can find many less than attractive people who have such a friendly, pleasing disposition that after getting to know them, you eventually feel you are in the presence of one of the most beautiful people in the world.

Unfortunately, ours is a jaded society. Ideal visions of beauty are constantly flashed at us from billboards, commercials and other media. We must be careful to separate reality from what we consider "perfection" and stop ourselves when we fall into the dangerous trap of expecting people in our "real" world to live up to expectations of the "perfect" image that we may have gotten from the media. Even if you still maintain that you would like a spouse who is beautiful, remember that outer beauty changes as we grow older. There is a bigger pay off if you keep your eye focused on the goal—to find someone whose values and character

> **Don't expect real people to live up to a "perfect" or idealized image.**

match yours—someone with whom you could live happily for the rest of your life!

A shadchan once told me a story of a couple whom he had set up which helped to put this whole issue into perspective for me. All the pieces of the shidduch had fit together; their backgrounds were similar, they had similar life-goals and they had all the makings of a yeshivishe couple. After the first date, the shadchan called up the girl for feedback on the date, and she replied, "I'm not interested." When the shadchan asked "Why?" The girl responded, "I'm not attracted to him." He asked her to explain what had turned her off, so that he would have a better idea of whom to set her up with the next time. She said simply, "I'm too embarrassed to tell you." The shadchan spent some time convincing her how it would benefit her to tell him what she didn't like so that he would be closer to the mark next time. She finally admitted, "He has premature silver-gray hair." It seemed that this bothered her to no end. She just couldn't get past this one issue. He asked her if they had had a nice time otherwise. She responded, "It was a terrific date. He's a great guy!" The shadchan made certain that, apart from the hair issue, everything else fit into place and he asked her to hold on while he called the boy and found out how the boy felt about the date. He told her he'd call her back later and they'd discuss the issue further.

The shadchan called the boy, and he said he had felt the date had gone extremely well. The shadchan called the girl back and said, "Let's talk about your concern. You are not attracted to him and that shouldn't be minimized; however, I am a big chasid of a second shot and if everything else was exactly what you were looking for, then I think you should give the guy another chance."

The second date became a third date and eventually there was a fourth date. After each date the shadchan called up the girl and said, "So, how do you feel about him?" She inevitably responded the same way. "He is exactly what I am looking for and we have a wonderful time together, but I still can't get past the hair thing." After every date it gnawed at her and she still hadn't made peace with it. He said, "Give it one more shot and that will decide it."

By the fifth date, when she called the shadchan, not a word about the boy's hair was mentioned. It just wasn't there. She just called to say that things were developing fantastically well and she was going to stick with it. Two months later they became engaged and were married five months after that.

While an attraction problem must be given serious consideration, this story illustrates how little details should not have undue importance. Try to always look at the bigger picture. If you get along, have similar values, really like each other and everything else fits together, try to look past a physical detail that may bother you. If you like someone and see them for who they are—for their full person—soon you will stop noticing what initially bothered you.

Action Steps

It's a good idea to reconsider when any of the following are your reasons for saying no:

1. The guy or girl was too nice or attainable.

2. No bells went off.

3. Really couldn't tell if you liked someone because it was too short a date.

4. Not enough feelings of attraction.

DEALING WITH REJECTION

However you look at it, rejection causes pain, humiliation, anger and hurt. No matter how tough you think you are, rejection is just one thing that will cut right through your veneer and leave your ego feeling bruised. It is one of those things that causes you to reel back and question your self worth. And this is an almost universal feeling! No one finds it easy to be rejected!

Before we discuss how to survive after you have been rejected you must know one important fact: *Every single person faces rejection at some point in their life.* You are not the only one who has gotten dumped! Even the seemingly "perfect" kids, the ones with all the *maalos* and all the *yichus* and the impeccable resumes, *each* and *every one* of them have had their share of rejection! It is just a fact of life and it must be dealt with. The key is accepting rejection and moving on.

Too many people become fixated on someone after being rejected by them, and this can seriously impact their future dating life. They may begin rejecting other people left and right in the hopes that one day the person who rejected them will change his or her mind and come running to them saying, "You're the one for me—I can't believe it took me this long to realize it!"

> **If someone rejects you it's best to cut your losses and love yourself enough to have the courage to move on.**

If this were a small problem, I would not feel the need to devote a full chapter to discussing it. However, the more I speak to people, the more I realize how many people have individuals in their life that they just can't get over. They'll hear their mother screaming in the background, "Rina, you are not getting any younger!" or "Chaim, what did you see in her anyway?" But they find that they just can't move on. They have become fixated in this molasses. Despite how smart, capable, frum, or attractive the people who they are set up with afterwards are—it doesn't make the slightest bit of difference.

Too many people stand in the way of their own happiness by not letting go of their fantasy of a certain person. They maintain a glimmer of hope that the phone will one day ring and this person will say, "I can't believe what a fool I was. You are the one I want to marry!"

Unfortunately, this is usually the stuff fantasies are made of.

The key is to become reality focused, cut your losses and love yourself enough to have the courage to move on. You might feel that your feelings for this person are so powerful that you are willing to wait until they see the light. However, you should find it in your heart to love yourself more and find a new light for yourself. Remember, people are resilient. Even after the biggest hardships, people can bounce back! And to survive the dating process you'll have to learn to be strong and resilient. No matter how painful and hurtful the rejection was, believe me, one day you will get over it and you will survive! One day you may even look back when you are happily married to someone else and have a good laugh. Remember, *anyone* who has taken risks has seen failure! Dating involves constantly taking risks—revealing your feelings and risking getting hurt—but it's the nature of the beast.

It always amazes me the extent to which people who have gone through tragedy can save face, pull together relatively quickly after their grieving and mourning, and start putting the pieces of their life back together. Their stubborn resilience to start getting back on track should be an inspiration to us all. And we should strive to be such great survivors.

When you're feeling hopeless and overwhelmed after a rejection, picture someone you know who experienced rejection and not only survived, but triumphed! Keep yourself on track and remember where you are headed. You can be sure that if someone said "no" to you, he or she wasn't the right one for you anyway.

The fact of the matter is, no matter how you slice it up, hearing a "no" after going out with someone you felt something

> **We are dating for <u>tachlis</u> purposes. No wonder there is such intensity, frustration and emotional involvement.**

for *is* deflating. The life of a shidduch dater is a fast-forwarded version of the secular dating world. There is no question that the entire experience of shidduchim is intense and difficult. I frequently overhear conversations taking place in college where a Jewish girl will come into class with a diamond ring on her finger and we'll all wish her Mazal Tov. Soon afterwards, one of the secular girls in the class will ask the famous question, "So how long did you know the guy for?" And the girl usually sheepishly answers, "about 4-6 weeks."

But there is nothing to be ashamed of! We are dating for *tachlis* purposes. And this is why there is such intensity, such frustration and such heavy emotional involvement. We're not going out just to go bowling, eat a good hamburger and do the same thing next week.

Our focus and purpose is solely to find the right person to marry. Once this is clear, there is no need to meander along and date for fun with no need for commitment from any of the parties. Our emotions are on full blast and we need to go full speed ahead. We get to know each other as deeply and broadly as possible during this time and continually think in terms of what we can develop from what we have here.

A shidduch date #3 typically occurs about two weeks after

knowing someone and can be equivalent to date #30 in the secular world, during which time they have known each other for six months. Shidduch dater are more vulnerable in their dating. Since the goal is to learn about a person quickly—and to find out more about anyone we have to give of our emotions and beliefs and hold nothing back. By the time the fifth date comes around, we've spent over twenty serious hours with this person, plus phone time. We have, hopefully, already established a strong rapport with this person and know a good deal about their likes and dislikes—their character and values. After forming this sort of intense connection with someone and getting rejected, one can really be hit hard.

Stages of Rejection

Here are some of the stages many experts say people go through after being turned down.

1. Denial—I don't believe they rejected me! He or she will surely change his or her mind.

2. Blame—You blame yourself and say, "If only I had been more animated, handsome, giggly, charming, interested, sophisticated, beautiful or hadn't worn that frumpy suit or made that stupid comment, he or she would have liked me."

3. Anger—After you have finished blaming yourself and you have laid on the guilt trip thick, you begin to feel terrifically angry toward this person for hurting you. You think to yourself, "Who was this person anyway, and how could they have done this to me?" The anger swells in you like a little volcano.

4. Sadness—At a certain point—hopefully—reality sets in and you start to see that this guy or girl is not calling back. You feel an authentic sense of sadness that it couldn't have worked out between you. Now is the time for the wishing and what ifs and the sadness that comes when you realize it was not meant to be. And it's ok to be sad—allow yourself this feeling!

5. Acceptance—Acceptance comes when you have finally gotten over this person enough that you can realistically see yourself married to someone else. You welcome each new date as a chance to find your potential soul-mate. You finally believe it is over with this person and you can go on with your life and put this person behind you.

While you might imagine, after being rejected, that you will never get to this acceptance stage—trust me, you will. Everyone has suffered rejection at some point in their life—although they may have had an easy time finding a shidduch, perhaps they had a hard time finding a job, or had little success at school. Life is easy for no one and with tefillah to Hashem to help you get over the rejection and with the proper amount of time, you will be able to move on and find someone better suited for you.

If you've been rejected here are a few things that I have discovered have helped others who had been rejected:

1. Reach Out To Friends. Call up a close friend. Share your feelings openly. It may feel embarrassing, but it helps if you can be reminded by those around you how wonderful, talented and likeable you are! You need a support network during this stressful period. Make sure you gather people around you who care about you and can help you as you date. This is not a time to feel proud! It takes strength to admit failure.

We all need to have our confidence rebuilt at a time like this. Having a close friend remind you that you are smart, good-looking, popular or fun to hang around with, can do wonders to boost your deflated ego! We all need to rebuild our confidence after being rejected. Good friends are like diamonds at a time like this, and you should turn to them to remind you of your positive attributes.

2. Rediscover Your Attributes. Pull out a mirror and take a long, good look at yourself—and I don't just mean your physical exterior. I mean look into your heart and at all the beautiful qualities that make you you. Think of some of the qualities people around you have appreciated. Perhaps you always serve your father tea on Friday nights or go out of your way to bring hot rolls for your mother from the bakery because you know how much she loves them. Perhaps you're a talented singer or a great student. Look at your eyes and how expressive they are—how they crinkle up when you smile and how they spill over with tears when your friend tells you something sad. We all have lovable characteristics. Every last one of us is gifted in some way and has qualities that would make someone happy in a marriage. It just takes each person a different amount of time to find their bashert. Although sometimes it may seem completely hopeless, keep your sense of humor and your love of life intact. Find the joy in your daily life—in the weather, in nature, in good friends or great music!

3. Try Laughter Therapy. Find a way to make yourself laugh. I know it helps me! I search for laughter in other people and believe the most beautiful thing on a person's face are the laugh lines that frame their eyes. I get my daily dose of laughter (a more powerful mood-lifter than anything a doctor can prescribe!) from a close friend who has a gifted sense of humor. Seldom a day goes by that I do not call her and see life for a few minutes through her quirky glasses. You can get a good laugh from a funny book, a close friend or even from within, by simply keeping your sense of humor.

4. Realize That No One Is Irreplaceable. Understand that the person you liked or thought you liked has qualities that you *will* find in another person. Perhaps the girl you liked had a fabulous sense of humor or a sunny smile or a sharp head on her shoulders. All these qualities can be matched in other people. Many girls and guys who got over someone and ended up marrying someone else, now have terrific marriages. They did what they thought they never would be able to do—they found someone who had many of the qualities they liked in the other individual—plus more. And even if the person they ended up marrying is missing a specific quality in one area, they may make up for it ten-fold in another area.

5. Focus On Other Things. Now is the time to turn your mind to other things. Set up a twice-a-week walking commitment with a friend. There is almost nothing as exhilarating as a brisk walk on a cool night with fresh air filling your lungs and your heart pumping as you briskly walk. Enroll in a local gym and swim twice a week or take an aerobics class. Or take a karate or Israeli dancing class. Now is the perfect time to take out a pair of roller blades or your old bike and take a ride to whatever park is in your neighborhood—try doing this with headphones and your favorite music—you'll find it can lift your spirits immeasurably.

Finding A Mentor

I cannot emphasize enough the importance of having a mentor during this time—this person can be a rav, trusted teacher, or savvy aunt, etc. who can guide you through times like these. It takes a mature person to admit that life is tough and no one can deal with everything by themselves. Having a mentor is dif-

> **Seek a mentor who has an understanding of Torah life as well as a knowledge of psychology and a good dose of insight into human nature and emotions.**

ferent than having a friend. A mentor cannot be replaced by a friend. A friend can be your cheering squad and take you out for a good time, but if you are looking for someone with a bigger, more global perspective who can help you move the process forward, you will need to find someone with years of life experience, someone who is savvy about dealing with relationships. The person you should seek as your mentor should be someone with an understanding of Torah life as well as a knowledge of psychology and a good dose of insight into human nature and emotions. It can be a rebbe or rebbetzin you respect. Or it can be a person you admire who lives on your block and with whom you may walk to shul every morning. The most important thing is that you respect this person and you trust them enough to confide in them.

Even if it's not comfortable to admit it, it's helpful to have guidance when you're young and making a lot of major, dramatic decisions about life. It's not easy finding and choosing someone you want to spend your life with. Sometimes our vision is shortsighted and we focus on things that are unimportant in the long run. What we need to find is someone who we trust and respect who can help us create a wider, more insightful vision. When you get rejected, for example, your instincts might be to recoil and allow the situation to eat away at you, but someone with a bigger, broader perspective can show you why you owe it to yourself to move on.

You might be thinking, I like this mentor thing but first of all—I have my pride (I don't want to feel I need help! Or I don't want anyone to know I need help!). Or perhaps you realize that no one has all the answers and you want to know how you can approach someone to make them your mentor.

I'll address the issue of pride first by clarifying a big mistake people make by confusing pride or ego with self-esteem. While pride or ego is *not* good, a healthy dose of self-esteem is exactly what we need to live a full, productive life. We have to work on getting over our pride because it can prevent us from doing many mitzvahs

> **We must become brutally honest with ourselves when we need help and find the courage to go out and get the help we need.**

and hold us back from getting where we need to in life. The human condition is such that we may feel we don't want to ask anyone for help. We don't want to admit we need help, and when we do need help we have great difficulty asking for it. We must become brutally honest with ourselves when we need help and find the courage to go out and get the help we need.

Ego or pride differs dramatically from self-esteem or self-worth. Self-esteem is feeling good about yourself and this is a crucial attribute. If you have a good self image, after you go out on a date you can call the shadchan and say, "I would like to go out with him again," even before you know the guy's opinion. If the guy says, "I'm not interested," your strong self-esteem will allow you to say to yourself "the reason he doesn't want to go out with me again has nothing to do with me because he didn't even know me! So on to the next!" If, on the other hand, you have no self-esteem or too much pride you'll feel sorry for yourself even if you didn't even like the girl or boy.

So once your pride or ego is out of the way and you're

ready to find a mentor you may wonder—how do I go about doing this? It says in *Pirkei Avos*, *"Aseh lechah rav uknei lecha chaver"*—"Accept for yourself a teacher and acquire for yourself a friend" (6:1).

When trying to find a mentor, the first thing to ask yourself is—is this the type of person I would like to become? Consider whether you would benefit from being around this person. Your mentor could be a hired relationship coach, a rabbi or a rebbetzin, or even someone in your community who you feel understands relationships.

> A mentor will be more than happy to help you. They will see it as an opportunity to give and spread Hashem's light.

Once you confirm that this person shares similar views about life, approach them and ask if they would mind if you discussed what's been going on in your life. Usually they will be flattered! Gauge your relationship with them—do they seem harried or preoccupied when you are talking, or do they seem attentive and happy to counsel you? Hopefully, you will be able to answer these questions in the affirmative and you will find yourself an invaluable asset: a role model who can guide you through dating years.

In most of the cases a mentor will be more than happy to help you. They will see it as an opportunity to give and spread Hashem's light. A mentor should take the time to meet with you in person and discuss your individual situation. It's best if you can feel open enough to reveal who you truly are as a person. This I refer to as Stage One: You must be open enough to allow them to point out you have this *maaleh* and that *maaleh*—that these things are there. A good mentor will focus on you and ask you to talk about yourself.

After you have established this, you can then go onto Stage Two which would be to deal more directly with how you feel. Let's say you were recently rejected. A mentor would guide you through your emotions and ask you, "How did it make you feel?" "How do you feel now?" They will help you analyze your emotions and ultimately point out that the best way to see this rejection is as a message from Hashem that this relationship was not meant to be. For some reason you had to date this individual, but they are not the one Hashem had in mind for you. By helping someone recover from rejection through support and discussion a mentor can build someone up again and give them the peace of mind to jump back full force into the dating scene.

Every situation must be dealt with individually. Some individuals need five minutes of "consolation talk" after they have been rejected and they can bounce right back and continue dating. For them the best thing is to immerse themselves into dating wholeheartedly and put the unpleasant situation behind them. Other people need to back off from dating for two or three weeks and take a breather. Whatever your needs are, a good mentor will help you achieve them, putting you back into focus so you can move on.

Action Steps

Deal with rejection in the healthiest possible way

1. Realize that everyone faces rejection at some point.

2. Don't stand in the way of your own happiness by obsessing about a someone who is clearly not interested in you.

3. Recognize that it's OK to feel deflated after getting a "no."

4. Be aware of the five stages many people go through after being let down: denial, blame, anger, sadness, acceptance.

5. Here are some things that work to get most people back on track:

   a. Reach out to friends.

   b. Rediscover your attributes.

   c. Try laughter therapy.

   d. Realize that no one person is irreplaceable.

   e. Focus on other things.

6. Find yourself a mentor.

PARENTS WHO MEAN WELL

One of the most stressful periods of life is the time spent looking for a shidduch. And although the shidduch dater may feel like it's only *they* who are stressed—parents are under almost equal pressure.

Think of your parents as your best friends. They pray for your success, try to give you the confidence to face obstacles and keep you in check when you have gone too far.

Parents, arguably even more than children, take their children's dating experiences seriously. They consider it their responsibility to marry off their children. At the bris, after a baby boy is born, the baby's father recites the words, "...*l'Torah, l'chupa ul'maasim tovim*—I will lead my child in the ways of Torah. I will walk him down the chupah and I will guide him to do righteous actions." Parents in the Jewish community are not *laissez-faire* about it. It's impossible for them to say, "So what if my daughter is 42 and not married. She has a

> **Parents sometimes need to be reminded that shidduchim are beyeidei shamayim (in the hands of G-d)…only G-d ultimately knows the best time for anyone to be married.**

great job in the city making $250,000 and she's happy. She has her own life." Jewish parents often feel so identified with their child that they consider their child's life their own life and they are all in this

together. Parents who are not fortunate enough to find a shidduch for a child often feel they have shortchanged the child terribly and sometimes even may feel they have failed as a parent.

This is just one of the many elements which make the dating situation so high-pressured. During the dating years it is often the primary source of all the stress between parents and children. Parents sometimes need to be reminded that shidduchim are *beyeidei shamayim* (in the hands of G-d). So while many parents might feel responsible if all their children aren't out of the house by age twenty-one, only G-d ultimately knows the best time for anyone to be married.

All those currently dating can attest to the fact that their parents take their dating life seriously—and personally. If a girl goes on a date and is rejected, she will have 150 rationalizations why the guy wasn't for her, even if she had all the plans in the world to say "yes" and already envisioned herself married to this guy and having five children with him. Once he says "no" she is immediately thrown into the situation of having to preserve her ego. This will cause her to find scores of reasons why he was all wrong for her. Suddenly his pants were too long and his eyes were in the wrong place. He was too confident or too insecure.

It's normal to do this in order to preserve your sanity and be able to continue to date others with a clear head. It's easier to believe that there was something wrong with your date— even if you really liked him or her before hearing the "no."

Parents, on the other hand, do not go on the date (I hope!). They do not know what transpired. They probably did not have a chance to pick up the irks and quirks of this guy or girl during the five minutes that they interviewed him. So when their daughter or son is rejected, they tend to take it personally. There is a tremendous amount of identification between parent and child (especially mother and daughter), and if somebody goes out with their child and then rejects him or her, it can be devastating to a parent. This is their child, their magnificent, beautiful, terrific child who has been rejected and they feel six times worse than the child who was rejected.

It helps to remember that parents mean well. They truly only want what will make their children happy. Often, however, in their quest to help their children forge a happy life they forget that each and every child has his or her unique identity. What is right for a parent, might not be right for each of their children. And what is right for one child may not be right for another child. A child might not necessarily want someone who is extraordinarily confident or rolling in dough even if parents believe these are admirable attributes. Many times children and parents don't see eye-to-eye concerning the profile of a suitable marriage partner. This problem can often cause intense strain while their child is dating.

> **Parents should take the time—before the whole shidduch process begins—to talk and create a united front concerning their goals for their child.**

In addition, many parents themselves, don't see eye-to-eye with each other when it comes to who their child's spouse should be. One parent might feel the young man should be learning in Lakewood for the first two years of marriage and the other parent may firmly believe he should immediately go to work after the wedding. One parent might believe that physical beauty is extremely important, while the other may insist that it is not. When two parents paint two entirely different pictures of what they feel would be perfect for their daughter or son, they confuse their child and make it extremely difficult for them to ever decide what type of individual they want for *themselves*.

We all want to please our parents and bring them *nachas*; we want them to feel proud of us and thankful to G-d for how we turned out. However, if parents are not unified in their opinion of what is "perfect" for their child, the child will feel confused or distraught—uncertain of how to please both parents at the same time. A child may even begin to feel discouraged, thinking that whomever they pick to marry, will ultimately make one parent proud of them and the other unhappy.

For this reason, it is crucial that parents take the time—

before this whole shidduch process begins—to talk and create a united front concerning their goals for their child. This is a high pressure moment for the person dating—parents at cross purposes can cause a child to never be able to make up his or her mind.

Before The Dating Process

As soon as someone feels mature enough to take on the responsibilities of running a house or supporting a family and is thus ready to be married, they should approach their parents with their decision and express exactly what they are looking for. This is a good time for parents to discuss their visions of the ideal husband or wife. It's also the perfect moment for the child to go through each point and characteristic brought up by their parents and consider if they too feel this is something they would like in a mate. If it isn't, a *calm* discussion should ensue, during which each side should explain why they do or don't feel this or that quality is important. Ultimately, many parents feel that their children are young and inexperienced, and perhaps do not know what is really best for themselves. However, parents should carefully assess what their children's specific needs are and be extra-cautious not to project their *own* needs.

The ultimate goal of this important discussion is to reach a compromise that will take the child's needs into account. A measure of a parent's real insight into their daughter or son's character is in place here.

Every human being has their own hang-ups and unique personality, and each and every one of us gets married for a slightly different reason. Some want a "cushy" life and therefore look

> **People marry for a multitude of different reasons and, if the same reasons are held by the two people getting married, it works out.**

for someone who can support them in style. Some fall in love and don't care about the consequences. Some are cerebral and orderly and everything has to make sense. Others view marriage as a logical transaction between two people who want to get married.

People marry for a multitude of different reasons and, if the same reasons are held by the two people getting married, it works out. It is not our place to judge someone who is getting married for what we perceive as less than the most idealistic of reasons. We do not know what lies in anyone's heart. The person they chose to marry, for whatever reason, may be exactly what they need to make them happy.

Rav Dovid Goldwasser suggests that parents take a closer look and ask themselves, "Do I really know and understand my child? What makes them happy? What makes them cry? What are their values? Which types of people will bring out the best in their child? Which personality will enhance their spiritual growth?"

In a comment concerning the relationship of Yaakov and Eisav with their parents (in *Bereishis*), Rav Shamshon Raphael Hirsch explains that a parent is responsible to know how to deal with each child respectively and how to guide them accordingly. The *Maharik* here discusses the importance of a parent helping to choose a life-long partner for their child based on who is best suited for their child, *not* necessarily who is best suited for themselves.

After these issues have been clarified, parents may proceed to the next step—helping to find the right *zivug* (soul mate).

A GUIDE FOR PARENTS

What Parents Should Do After The First Date

Once your daughter or son has the first date a number of things can happen:

a) She Or He Can Reject The Date.

This usually doesn't cause too much excitement. However, occasionally a parent may become angry and criticize their child for rejecting someone, saying things like, "You're crazy not to like this person! He or she is everything we want for you." It's dangerous for a parent to make such a definitive statement—by doing this a parent risks persuading their child to stop confiding in them about their dates.

A better approach: parents should make themselves conspicuously available after a date to openly discuss why their child thinks this individual was or was not a good match. Parents should be available as a sounding board or be available to offer helpful advice. Here your listening skills are crucial. If parents feel their child is making a wrong decision it's best *not* to just say "you're wrong." Instead it would be more productive to say, "We feel this boy is right for you because A, B and C." Through qualifying statements children may be more inclined to listen to the rationale behind parent's opinions. It's important that you're perceived to be a good listener. Ultimately, however, parents must try to trust their children's instincts and refrain from pressuring them into an uncomfortable situation.

The other problem for parents often arrives when:

b) Your Daughter Or Son Is Rejected.

Some parents make the mistake of blaming the victim. If their daughter or son goes out with three or four people and none of these people felt willing to have another date, parents may begin to blame their child. They may even say, "You're doing something wrong." Or they may be critical, mentioning that perhaps the child should've dressed better or talked less, talked more or have been more polite.

Instead of being there for their child when they most need support, (I must add here that most parents *are* good about this!) they may be tempted to become critical. Don't do it! Even if you don't say it outright you may give subtle suspicious signs— like saying "What did you do wrong that you were rejected by three people already?" Someone who has been rejected by a few people is usually already dismayed and upset with themselves— even if they don't show it! They don't need their parents to intensify these feeling of insecurity, hurt and depression.

Society encourages children to open up on dates (and you

112

have to open up on dates—you cannot subsist on conversations about the weather alone). Children are encouraged to reveal personal things about themselves, so when they are rejected, it can be devastatingly painful. This person knows *you*
and yet has rejected *you*. You gave this person a part of yourself and if the person didn't feel you were for him or her (especially if you liked this person) you feel double-crossed.

> The best thing you can do when your child is rejected is demonstrate your complete and absolute support.

The best thing you can do when your child is rejected is demonstrate your complete and absolute support. Be the one who helps to pump some confidence and positive energy back into your child. Be your child's cheering squad. Nurture and reassure him or her that the rejection has nothing to do with his or her worth as a person. The match was simply not meant to be.

Encourage your child to move on and continue to date other people and say that you're sure someone much better suited will be found. Your job is to be as supportive and helpful as possible. See the chapter "Dealing With Rejection" for some ideas on how to help your child recover from rejection.

Another thing many people have told me concerning the difficulties they have with their parents is the overemphasis some parents put on physical appearance while their children are dating. When your looks and the expense of your clothing are overemphasized, it can become dehumanizing, and many say it is a sign that we live in an increasingly superficial society.

We go through tremendous expense to dress children in a way that will catch admiring stares. This is a direct result of the tendency of passing judgment on people and sizing them up before they have even opened their mouths. We stand in awe of people, and say, "Wow, where'd she get that terrific suit?" while secretly plotting to search every fabric store in the borough in the hopes of creating one just like it. We spend too much of our time searching for the perfect thing to wear on the date, to the wedding, to the kiddush, etc. All the effort, time, and money spent searching for the perfect thing to wear can make a dating individual wonder if they do indeed have any value beneath the surface.

It would be helpful if the message that it is necessary to drop $1,000 on an outfit to a) look good, and b) get a guy, was changed. A young woman should be able to go into any store and choose a simple, classic suit and look beautiful in it. There is no need to make clothing the central focus of one's life.

One final thing many dating people have mentioned to me is that they find their parents overemphasizing wealth.

"Oh, so and so will have no problem getting married, the guy will just take one look at her D & B (Dun and Bradstreet report) and CV (curriculum vitae) and she'll be grabbed up," or, "she's so rich, they are all after her." Parents sit around the table and talk about this and that and don't realize that their kids are picking up every word. Children quickly learn to adopt parent's

114

attitudes and it goes a long way in making kids cynical and unhappy. Even if it *is* a fact, and even if it may be a reality in our society, it's better not to talk about it when your kids are awake; don't let your kids know that you are or even privy to this.

It is extremely undermining to discover that you are starting out on the shidduch scene with a handicap because your father doesn't own a bank. The feeling you should be relaying to your kids is that a sensible boy from a sensible family will be looking for a quality person and *not* a quality bank account—and that's the type of boy we want for you.

In summary, you want to be a positive force and stand firmly behind your children while they are dating. They need you as a confidante, as a friend and as an advisor. Open lines of communication between parents and children are more important now than ever. I know this is often difficult because kids sometimes think their parents, "just don't understand" and are on a totally different wavelength—my friend, for instance, told me she was convinced of this when her mother decided to send a bottle of ketchup and a package of sardines for *shalach manos* because she said it was practical.

However, even if there may be communication problems, work your best to show that from a parental point of view you are receptive to hearing what they have to say. You want to keep reminding your children that ultimately everything is in the hands of G-d. Encourage your children to have a positive attitude about dating and most importantly—that whomever they go out with, they should always enjoy themselves!

Action Steps

1. Message for parents: Don't forget that essentially shidduchim are in G-d's hands.

2. Parents identify with their children, and so, they will understandably take their child's dating life seriously.

3. Parents should take heed not to project their needs onto their child.

4. Parents should discuss what sort of spouse they think will be appropriate for their child, and then present their child with a unified opinion.

5. After a date, a parent's job is to be supportive and understanding of any decision a child may make. If they are in complete disagreement, a sensitive discussion should ensue.

6. If your child gets rejected, the worst thing you can do is blame him or her.

7. Emphasize your child—not his or her clothing!

8. During family discussions, avoid making blanket statements about someone else's bank account and the ease with which their children will find a shidduch as a result of this.

9. Be a positive force, standing behind your child and giving your child unconditional love when she or he is dating.

DO'S AND DON'TS FOR PARENTS OF SHIDDUCH DATERS

Parents play an important role in enabling their children to find an appropriate shidduch. I spoke with an astute mother who currently has children in shidduchim. She gave the following advice:

✦ **Put Your Child's Best Foot Forward.** Make sure that your son or daughter is always well-dressed and groomed. When you are with others, only speak well of your child (e.g., do not tell people that your daughter or son is on a diet or needs to be). Your child is in the spotlight, not you!

✦ **Emphasize Your Child's Special Attributes.** Learn how to say things about your child which make her appear special, not just nice. Every girl on the shidduch scene is sweet, attractive, nice and frum. You need something extra to make your son or daughter stand out.

Find something about your daughter that gives her a little spark above the rest, something that will help people differentiate her from all the other people in the crowd. "All the other girls that were recommended to my son were nice, sweet, had friendly dispositions—but I see Rina over here goes to Beth Israel Hospital every Sunday to visit the sick children—now this is something that might be worth pursuing."

> The truth is that, in a sense, the shidduch process resembles a fish market. No one is going to buy a fish that the owner says is ordinary.

The truth is that, in a sense, the shidduch process resembles a fish market. No one is going to buy a fish that the owner says is just ordinary—a nothing-special fish, i.e., a fish who graduated last in its class in fish school, perpetually annoyed the other fish and never did anything extraordinary in its life. But the fish which the owner wags at you and says, "Now here's a fish that's so tasty and sweet every mouthful will be a new adventure. Its flesh is so tender that it will make an instant fish-lover out of you." That is something that would really catch your attention!

As a parent you must imagine that you are the saleswoman and the stakes are much higher. Get creative and start discovering things about your children that will help them shine in a crowd. One woman described this to me as the "Frosted Cheerio effect." She claimed that she made sure each of her daughters had a special hobby. One was a great piano player and the other was an avid makeup artist and was always doing everyone's faces for the family simchas. She had even been sent to school to learn how to do facials and cosmetology, and she now had her own shop in the neighborhood with a steady clientele. This way, when she described her daughters to the mothers of perspective suitors, they would each be memorable and distinct and thus the name "Frosted Cheerio."

Never describe your child as "average." Within the realm of being honest about your child, be optimistic; i.e., if the glass is half full, don't describe it as entirely full, but don't describe it as half empty either. Here is a good time to add that you should avoid establishing your child as a four-star French chef if all the food she has ever made tastes like pet food—be honest and play up your child's positive side. Don't create a new and fictitious identity for your child—imagine the embarrassment when the in-laws come over to taste some of her famed cooking and she dishes up something which sends the entire family to the hospital with food poisoning.

✦ **Networking To Enlarge The Pool Of Candidates.** Enlarge your circle of acquaintances; never turn down opportunities to meet people. Advertise your child; attend every simchah and every function you are invited to.

Now is not the time to become the social recluse you have always dreamed of becoming! Now is *not* the time to stop attending tzedakah teas or PTA luncheons. Now is the time to get one of those nifty weekly planners and start filling it up with activities, luncheons, and parties where you can enlarge your circle of acquaintances and give your children more exposure.

Donate your tzedakah money to the appropriate institutions. For example, if you are looking for a Chaim Berlin boy, make sure the yeshivah is high on your tzedakah list and you're attending functions at that school.

✦ Avoid Any Bad Publicity During This Sensitive Time. On the other hand, think carefully before you allow the institution to honor you. By being honored as a donor to one institution, you are alienating those who don't like the institution. As a rule think twice before you allow yourself to stand out in any way. The same applies for having your name in the news for good or bad. Inevitably this will arouse strong opinions and judgments about who you are which are not necessarily accurate and can possibly cut off possible contacts.

✦ Don't Discount Anyone As A Shadchan. Anyone can be a shadchan—your grocer, your child's teacher or professor, even the person your child went out with. No one is too unimportant for your child (or you) to make a good impression on and for you to ask if they know of a good candidate for your child.

✦ Don't Ever Antagonize A Shadchan. You will not get along with every shadchan, but in such cases, it is far better not to call them back than it is to antagonize them.

✦ Persistence Pays Off. Be persistent with a shadchan and call him/her on a regular basis, even if they never seem to have anyone for you. The squeaky wheel gets the grease.

✦ Keep Your Feet On The Ground. Be realistic about your child's expectations. For example, it is unlikely that a doctor will be interested in your daughter if she never went to college. Or that your son will marry a rich girl if he is neither rich himself nor a good student.

✦ **Don't Research Each Shidduch Too Much.** Comprehensive research before a date should not be necessary, nor is it particularly helpful. If you cannot get information about someone from a few simple phone calls, that is a warning signal and you should probably not pursue it further. Information should be readily available about any young man or woman who lives in frum society, particularly if they give you the references.

✦ **Allow Your Child To Find Someone Good For Them <u>Not</u> Necessarily Good For You.** Within reason, try not to impose your preferences on your child if the child does not share these preferences. Although you are older and wiser, it's impossible to tell your child what is attractive to them and what is not—this is a highly personal and subjective matter.

✦ **Respect Your Child's Decisions.** Always respect the reasons your child gives for rejecting a prospective shidduch. Remember that even if the reason your child is citing sounds superficial, if your child liked the person, the superficial drawback would be easily overlooked. Sometimes what may be bothering your child is something that he or she cannot articulate, and your child is choosing instead to focus on what might seem "picky" to you. In any case, you know your own child and thus you will know what kind of decision-maker he or she is.

✦ **Be Prepared.** Before the date, make sure that you, your spouse, and your house are all in tip-top shape. At least one parent (or sibling if need be) should be on hand for any last-minute hysteria, missing safety pins, cleanliness inspection, etc.

Action Steps

1. Put your child's best foot forward.

2. Make your child sound special whenever you mention him or her.

3. Enlarge your circle of acquaintances.

4. Think twice before you allow yourself to stand out.

5. Be aware that anyone can be a shadchan.

6. Don't ever antagonize a shadchan.

7. Be persistent with a shadchan—remember the squeaky wheel gets the grease.

8. Be realistic about your child's expectations.

9. Comprehensive research before a date should not be necessary.

10. Within reason, try not to impose your preferences on your child.

11. Always respect your child's reason for rejection.

12. Before the date, make sure you, your spouse, and your house are in tip-top shape.

TO SAY OR NOT TO SAY– THAT IS THE QUESTION

One of the most prickly areas of shidduchim is *loshon horah*. How do you convey what may be important information about someone you know without breaking the laws of *loshon horah*? When it comes to shidduchim, the strength of our words is incomparably powerful. One slight, off-handed comment said without thinking can entirely ruin a shidduch. At the same time, withholding information or neglecting to mention something that should be disclosed can ruin someone's life.

If you are asked to give information about a shidduch, you must be aware that the information giver has the most influential role in the shidduch process. You are dealing with life and death issues and therefore each word said should be weighed carefully, with complete awareness of the power you have to affect someone's life. You must be extra careful not to abuse this power.

In *Mishlei* it says, "*lev tzaddik yehegeh la'anot*—a tzaddik thinks before he or she talks" (15:28). This is not the time to talk impulsively and rashly about anyone! Once a word is uttered it is indelible and the impression may be everlasting. Therefore, even if you are required to disclose information about another individual, do so with discretion.

> **Even if you are required to disclose information about another individual, do so with discretion.**

We all have shortcomings and faults—it's unnecessary to focus on them. G-d is the ultimate "seer." He sees humans with all their shortcomings and flaws and after all that He still says, "*Me ke'amcha Yisrael, goy echod ba'aretz*—Who is like the nation of Israel, there is only one people like this in all the land" (*II Samuel* 7:23). We should attempt to model this behavior. It is time to take our roles seriously and realize the indelible impact our words can have on listeners.

The Five Conditions

There are five conditions to take into account before deciding if you are permitted to disclose negative information about someone:

1. It's a fact. You must be 100% sure that the information you are disclosing is factual. No speculation or inference is permitted. You must have first-hand knowledge that what you are saying is absolutely true. Much of the information you may be inclined to relay may be merely your personal judgment and opinions. These kinds of things are not based on facts and thus we are prohibited from saying them.

We are seldom 100% sure about anything. Therefore, carefully consider reporting something even if you have witnessed it with your very own eyes. If, for example, you tell someone a guy is "cheap" based on a date you had with him last year when he didn't tip the waitress sufficiently, please consider that he may have a) changed his nature since then, or b) been short on cash after he paid for the dinner.

2. There's a good reason to disclose the information. The information you will be disclosing must be "*letoeles*," or for a good purpose. There must be something definite that can be accomplished with the words you will be saying—don't just vent your frustrations because you are upset that someone rejected you (or rejected someone you know). If the shidduch will be finalized regardless of what you will say, your input has *no* purpose and therefore the information you may think of disclosing is prohibited—and is an outright violation of the laws of *loshon horah*.

3. If you can find a way not to disclose, don't! If there's anything in your power that can be done to stop the shidduch without necessitating the disclosure of this piece of information, it would be prohibited to say it. If you know, for example, that the boy you are being asked about has a harsh temper, and you know the girl comes from a soft-spoken easygoing family and would never be able to handle a husband who loses his cool easily, than you might simply put it as, "The boy is not for her," as long as you are sure they will listen to your advice and not go through with the shidduch. You can also say something along the lines of "*Adam tov chaver ra*" (meaning he's a nice guy and a real mentch but he would not be compatible with her).

> Be discerning about every word that leaves your lips. Realize the powerful impact that your words can have on others' lives.

4. Only say what you must. Not a word more. When you have real facts to report and you are sure your words will accomplish something and you are unable to stop the shidduch from taking place any other way, remember: weigh every word as if you were giving away your own hard earned-money to an enemy. Be careful not to embellish or add anything just for the sake of feeling important or being admired in this person's eyes as someone who has the power to make or break a shidduch. You will be admired much more if you are discerning about each and every word that leaves your lips and you realize the powerful impact that your words can have on others' lives.

5. Don't say anything that will cause unnecessary harm. If the derogatory information that you will be communicating will cause someone unnecessary damage, then don't say it. For example, let's say you know for a fact that the boy you are being asked about is having trouble with his business and you know that the girl's family is looking for someone who is financially well-off. You also know that if you disclose this information to the girl's father, not only will the shidduch definitely be over but so will the boy's financial future if word of his failing business gets around. In this case, the derogatory information should be withheld and one should seek an alternative means of getting the message across that this boy may not be for her.

Here's a short, cute pneumonic to help you remember the five conditions mentioned above so that next time you give information for a shidduch you can easily recall them and decide if what you want to say is better off being withheld:

With—**Weigh** each word.

Feelings—**Facts**, make sure what you are saying is 100% factual.

People—**Purpose**—you must have a purpose and accomplish something with your words.

Are—**Alternative method**—see if you can try to stop the shidduch in a way that doesn't necessitate *loshon horah*.

Extra—**Excess damage**—if the information would cause more damage than it has to—don't say it.

Careful.

With feelings—make sure you know the strength of your words before you say them.

EHR HAT GEZUKT, ZI HUT GEZUKT

Dating is like an enormous puzzle or mystery novel. Every action is analyzed, every word scrutinized. You're looking for insights into character and personality. You wonder what everything means as you learn about someone.

But sometimes you may be misunderstanding something. You think something your date has done expresses one thing when they were actually trying to express just the opposite. I did a little investigation into twelve central concerns that people have while they are dating. I obtained the male and female perspective on each concern.

Remember—these opinions are not in any way written in stone! But they may provide some insight! And they may help you realize that not everything is as it appears to be! Here we go!

1. A boy takes you to a lounge—
What does that say?

Boy's Opinion: Confucius say: Man who take girl to lounge is cheap. End of story. I never take girls to lounges because I'm a stern believer in Confucius.

Also, if you go to a lounge you have to sit there for two to three hours and make conversation the entire time. Plus there is usually a one hour ride to get there and back during which you must also make conversation the entire time. That's five solid hours of talking to someone you don't know! Let me tell you, that is really tough! Also a lounge doesn't lend any spontaneity. There's nothing to break up the monotony. There's nothing happening in a lounge. All you can do is just stare at each other. There's no environmental stimulus for the conversation. In contrast, a restaurant usually has interesting people and food that deserves comment and that automatically adds to the conversation.

Girl's Opinion: Some girls are O.K. with a lounge because they are uncomfortable eating in front of guys, but the guy should be on the lookout for a girl's expression when he says he's taking her to a lounge. If her response is, "A LOUNGE?" and she gives him a look that says she'd rather spend the evening cleaning a drain, he should rethink his plan!

2. If the date is called for 6:00 p.m. and the door-bell rings at 6:00 p.m. what does that means?

Boy's Opinion: It means that the guy is punctual. He had his finger on the doorbell at 5:59 and a half and he's a good man. A man on time is worth your time. Girls who think that guys are "nerdy" if they come exactly on time are wrong in their assumption! A real gentleman is respectful of a girl's time and never keeps her waiting. If the date was called for 6:00, he should be there at 6:00.

Girl's Opinion: He's prompt, he makes a point of being there on time. It's a good thing. It shows he's interested. One thing though, a guy should *never* arrive early.

3. What does that mean if a guy is fifteen minutes late ?

Boy's Opinion: He probably has a good excuse like traffic or his goldfish died. Something must have come up and you should forgive him. If he has a car phone, though, he should give her a call. I run into traffic all the time so I know to leave my house 45 minutes before a date even if the girl lives two blocks away. I turn the corner and suddenly I hear the sirens going WOOUU WOOUU and there's a police car and fire truck rushing my way and my car is blocked in from all sides. So, you definitely want to leave yourself ample time to get there.

Girl's Opinion: If he is fifteen minutes late he probably has a good excuse. A guy doesn't have to call, unless he's more than fifteen minutes late. Once, a guy was supposed to be at my house at 6:00 p.m. At 6:00 he doesn't show up and he called and told me, "Hi, I'll be there at 7:30." (Oh well, at least he called!)

Boy's Opinion: I had a similar story. I told the girl I'd be three hours late. I told her to take her shoes off and make herself comfortable!

Girl's Opinion: What happened? Did you miss the plane or something?

Boy's Opinion: I missed her house by about 30 miles.

4. How do you feel about telling a girl or being told where you are going before the date?

Boy's Opinion: I think a girl should be informed where she is going. I'm not offended if a girl asks "Where are we going?" or even if she gives me some options about where she'd like to be taken.

Girl's Opinion: I really like it when a guy tells me where we will be going in advance. This way I know how to plan. One guy called, (actually it was the same person who called up at 6:00 and said he would be there at 7:30) and I asked him, "I wonder where we're going because I'm dressed kind of formally." He said, "Don't worry, I'm sure you are dressed appropriately," and as much as I repeated my concern, he kept saying, "I gotta go, but I'm sure you're dressed appropriately." I found this unhelpful. Most girls do like a little notice about where they'll be going so they will be dressed appropriately.

5. What exactly is a "list" and why is it almost exclusively a male phenomenon?

Boy's Opinion: Let's say a boy has been seeing a girl for a while. This is usually when all the phone calls from the shad-chanim come in with other prospects. So, while Chaim is dating Suri, he gets *"red"* (this means he is suggested to other girls) to Chani, to Chava Rifkie, Chana Raisy and all the names start piling up. What most boys do is date the person who came up first on the list first and the last one last. You asked why guys usually have the lists. Well, my mother has a theory that a guy can be 21 years old and older and they have all the time in the world, but as soon as a young woman turns 21 she begins to panic. The shadchanim tend to adopt these girls and *"red"* them to many boys simultaneously, so they end up on a few lists at the same time.

Girls Opinion: Girl's just don't have lists. I never heard of a girl who has a list. It just doesn't happen. Statistically they say there are more girls than guys. In fact, a girl telephoned me and told me that the shadchan who usually sets her up is, "short on men." My friend thought the shadchan meant she has only short men, but no, she was, "short on men."

Boy's Opinion: Yeh, the shadchanim tell me that too, "I have tons of girls. Beautiful girls, wonderful girls—no boys."

6. A boy takes a girl to a lounge and then afterwards he asks her if she would like to get something to eat and she says "No."

Boy's Opinion: To a guy this means that she's not interested in him and that she doesn't want to spend any more time with him. Many guys will take this as an affront. By asking her to the restaurant, the guy is signaling that he wants to spend money on her. Her rejection of the restaurant means that she doesn't want him to spend the money and is not interested in him. If she is really interested then saying no to a restaurant invitation sends a confusing signal.

Girl's Opinion: You are reading too much into when a girl says "no." It simply means that she's not hungry. That's it. Guys always think that women don't say what they mean. I went out with this psychologist recently and no matter what I said, he thought I meant something else. He came to my house in a big yellow taxi cab. He waited in front of my house and he asked me, "Do you know the quickest way to get on to the BQE (Brooklyn-Queens Expressway)?" I thought I did, but it turned out that I really didn't. My luck, we got lost and the meter was running! We ended up on Clara Street somewhere. I felt really bad and the taxi driver was looking really nervous, so I said, "It's late, why don't we just stay in Brooklyn already." So we ended up staying in Brooklyn.

At the end of the date the guy told me: "I don't think you wanted to stay in Brooklyn because you felt bad about the meter. You wanted to stay in Brooklyn because you didn't like me. You didn't want to travel all the way to Manhattan with me." He had totally misinterpreted my comment—I really didn't mind going at all!

Often you just have to take what someone says at face value: if a girl says "no" to dinner this probably means she's not hungry.

7. A man goes out with a woman and he doesn't call the shadchan back right away.

Boy's Opinion: A guy (or a girl) should call the shadchan in the morning regardless of the answer. After a guy drops off his date, he's got plenty of time to think. Even if he lives in the same neighborhood, one night should be enough time to come to a decision.

Girl's Opinion: If he doesn't speak to the shadchan within a day "the guy's not a mentch." You can't imagine how much it destroys someone's week to be in limbo. Even if the answer is "no" at least a woman has closure and can go on.

8. Who should the shadchan approach first if he has a name for a shidduch, the girl or the boy?

Girl's Opinion: Definitely the boy. I don't want to have to find out about a boy, get my hopes up only to find out they haven't even *"red"* it to him yet and when they finally do, "he's busy." I think guys are generally the calmer of the two. Therefore a shadchan should approach them, get their answer and then approach the girl. If I hear about a guy first, I know I'll sit for a week biting my nails thinking that the guy is stalling and still hasn't gotten back to the shadchan with an answer. If a guy receives a name first and says "yes," he'll wait for a few days for the girl's answer and the waiting probably won't phase him too much. Besides, a guy usually has a few things going on at the same time. So if one doesn't work out it's not the end of the world. A girl, on the other hand, will often make herself sick thinking about what his answer will be.

I want to know when a guy is told about me that he has already said "yes" and is ready to go on a date. Otherwise, I don't want to hear about it.

Boy's Opinion: I think society is strange and unfair. Stereotypically they'll ask the guy first if he's interested in order to protect a girl's feelings. This is strange because guys have feelings too. We're just as human and we get our share of "no's." I think a shadchan should talk to whomever they know better and have a greater commitment to!

9. When a girl says, "I had a nice time" after a date, what does this mean?

Girl's Opinion: It means she honestly had a good time, not necessarily that she wants to see the guy again. It's a matter of social etiquette. It's not misleading to say this because in all honesty one might have had a nice time. However, just because a girl did enjoy herself, this doesn't necessarily mean that she wants to see someone again.

Boy's Opinion: I agree with her. I don't think that a girl has to mean it when she says she had a good time. I don't mind if she doesn't mean it. I personally like to hear it. If I take someone out, probably to a good restaurant, and spend my time and money to treat her well, it's gratifying to hear some sort of verbal reciprocation. I won't feel slapped in the face if she says, "no" after that.

Girl's Opinion: I would say "I had a nice time" either way. However, there are a few different types of "no" that one can receive after a date. There's the "no" to a guy who takes out his calculator watch to figure out the tip. And there's the "no" to the guy who treated you well and took you out to the bowling alley at Chelsea Piers and then to a nice dinner. Each "no" is different. One is the "sorry-you're-cheap-no," while the second is the, "I-had-a-very-nice-time-but-we-wouldn't-work-out-together-no." You really have to know your "no's"!

10. What do you think when a previous date of yours calls you up and says, "I wasn't for you, but I know a great girl or guy who would be perfect for you?"

Boy's Opinion: I have to admit I would question the motives. I would really wonder what's going on in her mind—it didn't work out with us and now your "*redding*" me to someone else—what's going on? First you are out of my life and then you mysteriously pop back into my life for some reason. I would wonder, do you want me for someone else because you *did* like me or because you *didn't* like me? I should add that whether or not I could figure out the motives and regardless of what these motives might be, I'm inclined to think that this previous date probably means well and I would take her suggestion seriously.

Girl's Opinion: I would question the person's motives, but I, too, would check into it and give it a chance. One guy who I essentially rejected, called me up afterwards to set me up with his friend. I wondered whether he was angry at me for rejecting him. I thought he would have a little picture of me on his wall to throw darts at. Initially, I did think that he was trying to get back at me by setting me up with someone with little devil ears coming out of his head! But I also thought that it was possible that he would have someone for me whom he thinks would be more appropriate—I really wasn't sure!

I did know a friend who had gone out with a guy and even after he said "no" to her, she still liked him for a while after that. She thought that the way to maintain a connection to him was to set him up with other girls and this way they'd be in contact. She hoped that this way there would be a chance he'd reconsider dating her. So sometimes there's a method to this madness. So always tread carefully and question why this person whom you rejected or who rejected you is now so eager to get back into your life. But in most cases I would go out with someone suggested to me by someone I rejected.

I have heard two clichés concerning this:

"Don't throw out—recycle." Or my personal favorite: "When in doubt—go out."

11. Do you think that a shadchan should be totally honest?

Boy's Opinion: A shadchan just called me up recently. I happen to prefer petite girls and she didn't know that.

She told me "I have a perfect girl for you! She's tall, she's nice, she's skinny, beautiful, wonderful."

And I said, "Well, you know, I prefer girls who are kind of small."

She said, "Oh, she's small, she's small, she's not so tall. She's perfect."

Before I could say, "What?"—Boom! She had already changed her mind.

This shadchan is really good. She can *"red"* me ten girls in a second. She goes, "Oh, I have one girl from school A, and another one who's a genius—she's so beautiful, tomorrow she's flying in from Mexico, and I have another one from New Jersey." I once asked her, "Who did you just *"red"* me?" I was sitting there with a pen and I wrote down a big "T" on my paper because I thought I heard that was one of the girl's names. And she's like "Pick one quick! They are wonderful, wonderful! You can't let them go!"

A shadchan should definitely be honest. It doesn't make any sense not to be completely frank! You'll find out the truth anyway. I'm 5 ft 8½ inches, and let's say the girl is 5 ft 3 inches. The shadchan's going to make me 6 ft tall and the girl 4 ft 7 inches. But we are going to end up with the same height difference anyway! So there's no reason to lie about it.

Girl's Opinion: A shadchan should definitely be honest. Beauty is subjective. What people find attractive is quite personal. You never know what someone will find attractive, so there's really no reason for a shadchan not to be honest. I think a shadchan can really end up hurting someone's feelings by not being honest.

A friend of mine was 21 years old and her absolute age limit was 29. The shadchan called her up about a guy she claimed was 29. Perfect, she thought. So she checked into it and said "yes." They made a date and soon after the shadchan called back and said, "I made a mistake, the guy is really 32." The girl didn't know what to do. She wanted to say "no" right away but the shadchan felt—once you make the date you have to keep your word. So they went out and the guy liked the girl a lot. After the date she said "no" for the same reason—she felt 32 was too old for her. The boy was really hurt. A little honesty at the beginning can save hurt feelings later on. If you know there is something a person will not compromise on (i.e., a certain build, age, background) there is no reason to lie about it since they will probably not change their mind about it later on.

12. How do you feel if your date compliments you?

Girl's Opinion: I think a girl appreciates a compliment *if it's in good taste*. You can compliment something general like her blouse, sweater or jewelry and she will usually take it well. It's nice to be noticed and saying something complimentary can make someone feel a stronger connection to you. But be careful to seem to notice everything about the girl or this will embarrass her.

Boy's Opinion: Compliments go a long way with a guy! If you compliment me on my job or my personality, I would appreciate it!

However, as far as complimenting a girl, I know it's sensitive and it's best to be cautious. As a rule, it's probably better to stay away from spontaneous compliments that just pop into your head, but rather give it some thought beforehand to avoid discomfort. I know I once took out a girl who was insecure about having chipped her tooth while ice skating. I took the cue and after giving it some thought I told her, "You have a beautiful smile." She was insecure, and I wanted to make her feel better about it and boost her self-confidence.

Action Steps

1. Come on time to a date—it signifies a great deal about your character (like that you are considerate about other people's time!).

2. A guy should inform a girl in advance where she will be taken during the date—she'll appreciate it.

3. A "list" is actually a number of girls being set up with a guy at one time. He is usually busy seeing someone while this is happening, so the names pile up.

4. A guy shouldn't be insulted if a girl rejects his offer to buy her dinner. She simply may not be hungry.

5. Call the person who set you up immediately after the date (i.e. the next morning).

7. Surprise! Surprise!—Guys have feelings too, and a shadchan might want to switch off and sometimes mention the shidduch to the girl first.

8. It is appropriate and polite for a girl to say, "I had a nice time" after a date, regardless of whether or not she wants to see the guy again.

9. If you have someone you want to suggest to an ex-date, be ready to answer the question, "Why do you think he/she is for me if you weren't for me?"

10. Attention shadchanim: girls and guys really appreciate your honesty!

11. A compliment, given in good taste and coming from either a girl or a boy, can go a long way.

STORIES THAT WILL MAKE YOUR DATING LIFE LOOK GOOD

All names in the following stories have been changed to protect the identity of the people involved! Now sit back, relax and enjoy the stories.

And You Thought Your Date Was Cheap!

It was a mercilessly hot summer day, the kind of day when you don't know what to do with yourself once you are outside, except maybe run back in. What must be the world's cheapest man shows up for the date and takes a girl for a lovely sweat-filled walk around Central Park. After two hours the girl was famished, soaked with sweat, and so thirsty she salivated every time they walked by a soda machine, yet he offered nothing. Although she could have paid for her own soda she was curious about why he didn't offer. Finally, she announced, "I'm really thirsty, could you please buy me a drink?" They returned to a soda machine, and he inserted four quarters, and handed her the drink of her choice. As she sipped the soda, she glanced at him and thought, "Maybe there's hope." But then she noticed out of the corner of her eye that he was watching her enviously as she gulped down the cold, refreshing drink. "Aren't you thirsty?" she asked. He replied, "Well, yeah, you're not going to drink all of that yourself are you?"

Tongue-Tied

Listen, it was his first date and the guy was nervous, so cut him some slack on this one. Anyway, after tilting and retilting his hat in the mirror forty times and tying and retying his tie knot until it was just so, he was finally ready to go out. It suddenly occurred to him that he had no idea what he was going to talk about with this girl and so he began to panic. His mother took one look at his distressed state and realized she had better do something quick or she'd never get her son out the door. She ripped a sheet of paper out of a notebook and jotted down a list of ten questions to ask the girl, including: What school did you go to? How many brothers and sisters do you have? How do you like your job? So he grabbed the list and headed out the front door to pick up his date.

While he was driving in the car with the girl, whenever the conversation grew sparse, he would sneak a look at the questions from his mother's list. At one point, he got so nervous that he handed the paper to the girl and said, "Here, why don't you read these questions and answer them!"

Mr. Cool

It was her first date and his 200th. He was cool, calm, and absolutely in control. She was tense, jittery, and her nerves were about to snap. It was the big numero-uno, and the way it was going in her family, this was going to be the one. She was sure she had done adequate research and he had come out completely clean—this guy was what you call quality. The guy showed up, took one look at the nervous wreck that he had intended to date, and he decided to have some fun. After all, he thought to himself, she looks like she could use a little loosening up. So, after she got into his car he turned to her and asked, "Soooo, when do you want to get married?" The girl took one look at him, threw up all over the car and ran out. The date was over in less than two minutes!

The Silent Boy

A friend recently got set up with a guy. The shadchan gave her a glowing report about the guy and ended with a little, harmless phrase, "But there's just one thing..." "Uh Oh," she thought to herself. "There's always just one thing. What's it this time? He has a chronic post nasal drip? He's 44 years old, or five-foot-four? She braced herself for what was coming. The shadchan continued, "There's one little thing and that is he doesn't like to make phone calls. He doesn't want to call; he's tired of being prejudged from the phone call alone. So, I'll make the date for the two of you and he'll just show up."

"This gives new meaning to the words 'blind date,'" my friend thought to herself. "How do I know who's going to show up at my door? Maybe it'll be an evil impostor! What time should I tell him to arrive? How should I dress? This is ridiculous! There must be some way I can get in contact with this guy! Can I fax him? If he should happen to want to go out with me a second time, will he call me then?"

Don't worry too much about what happened because there was no second time. As a matter of fact, to the best of my recollection, there was no first time either!

Call the Cohen

A man arrived for a date and saw a nicely set table. He waited for a few moments at the table for the girl to come down. Finally a woman came in, shaitel and all, and began talking to him. He figured this must be the girl's older married sister who would be entertaining him until his date showed up. He asked her her name and to his utter disbelief she gave the same name as the girl he was supposed to be going out with. He went into visible shock. She picked up on it right away and asked, "Didn't they tell you I'm divorced?" to which he replied, "Didn't they tell you I'm a Cohen?"

Only For The Special Girls

Casually she looked through *The Jewish Press* personal ads one day and saw an advertisement that piqued her interest.

The ad was for a shadchan whose motto was, "Every special person needs a special date." "Maybe this shadchan is different," she thought. "Maybe this shadchan is hoarding all those eligible bachelors." She called up the shadchan and said she had gotten her number from a newspaper and was interested in being set up. The shadchan replied, "The ad said every *special person*—we only set up physically or mentally handicapped people!"

You're Dismissed

A man went to pick up his date at her school. He planned to take her to a nearby place for a soda. Instead she invited him into one of the college lecture halls. He followed her and she sat at a desk across from him and proceeded to shoot question after question at him. During the interview, which lasted for approximately three hours, she covered everything, including whether he would eventually want to live in Israel, and where he planned on sending his unborn children to yeshivah. She asked him about his lifelong goals and demanded where he could see himself in five years. Three hours after the interrogation had begun she excused herself and said to her date that he could go. One week later, he received a call from the shadchan, who said, "The girl wasn't interested, but she has a friend who would be perfect for you." The guy said "no" initially, but later changed his mind and agreed to go out with the girl's friend. "After all," he said, "she knows more about me than I know about myself!"

Holy Socks

A guy and a girl went bowling on a date. As soon as he had finished paying for her game and her bowling shoes, she recalled a gigantic hole in her right sock, from which her big toe mercilessly stuck out. He turned to her and asked, "Can I have your shoe?" She needed to stall for time, so she said, "No." He was surprised and replied, "What do you mean no, you have to give me your shoe! You can't bowl without bowling shoes!" She racked her brain to think of something quick and retorted, "It's not *tzniusdik*! If you want me to give you my shoe, you'll have to turn around!" He turned around and she quickly fixed her sock to cover up her big toe. She was ready to bowl.

Ivy-League Here We Come

He was an exceptionally bright guy with a superb control of the English language. Every time he opened his mouth to speak, the girl felt like a complete air head. She made her best effort to remain quiet so at least he would think she understood what he was talking about. He told her about the business he was running with his two partners and added that this coming week was going to be a difficult week. His exact words were, "This week will be a critical juncture for all of us." She sat there perfectly silent and just nodded, thinking to herself, "The last time I heard those words spoken was during the President's inaugural address."

He seemed to pause and looked at her for a response. She

blurted out, "Yes, I know exactly what you mean, I have those critical junctures all the time, it must be really rough for you."

Sometimes you just have to be fast on your feet!

As Long As You Wear A Hat On Top Of Your Shaitel

A shadchan from Williamsburg called a girl I'll call Miriam. As soon as Miriam heard who it was she thought, "I'm not the Williamsburg type, why is she calling me? It's true my father wears a *streimel* and I live in Borough Park, but Williamsburg is a far stretch." The shadchan said the boy had only one request—he wants the girl he marries to wear a hat on top of her shaitel.

She thought to herself, "I probably would, if that's what my husband wanted." So she told the shadchan, "I think I would, but does the boy know I graduated from college and have my B.A."

The shadchan replied, "The boy doesn't mind, as long as you will wear a hat on top of your shaitel."

She responded, "Does he know I am getting a master's in English literature from Hunter College?"

The Shadchan replied, "Fine, fine, as long as you'll wear a hat on top of your shaitel."

The girl responded: "Does he know I belong to the Jewish Defense League?"

The shadchan again replied, "Don't worry, he'll understand, as long as you'll wear a hat on top of your shaitel."

The girl again revealed another side of herself: " But does

he know I was in prison for demonstrating for Soviet Jewry?"

Again the shadchan said, "That's fine, as long as you'll wear a hat on top of your shaitel." She thought to herself, she could be the uni-bomber for all this woman cared, but the guy wouldn't mind. He might not even notice—*as long as she wore a hat on top of her shaitel!*

What Was That You Said?

A girl once received a call from a shadchan who wanted to set her up with a baal teshuva who she said had a "colorful" background. The girl was excited since the baalei teshuva she had dated had all been open-minded, worldly, interesting people and she had especially enjoyed herself on those dates. She immediately said "yes." Later that week, they spoke and agreed to meet at a coffee shop in Manhattan.

The conversation went well. After they spoke for a while they began discussing his experience as a baal teshuva. She decided to be direct and asked him, "When did you first become a baal teshuva?" He responded, "In prison." She figured he must have been imprisoned for embezzling money or something like that. To reassure herself she asked, "What for?" He replied, "For murdering my last girlfriend." Her eyes nearly popped, but she looked at him, as if to say, "Yup, this is a perfectly normal occurrence. I sit across from murderers every day." But in the back of her mind, she scanned the restaurant furiously for the nearest exit. It turned out that when the shadchan said colorful, she had meant it. This guy had literally spent time in prison for killing someone. After years of soul searching behind the prison bars, he had come to religion. He then explained to her in detail why he had killed a woman and how he had come to regret what he had done. She listened, thanked him politely for sharing with her this wonderful, beautiful story, and whisked out the back door as fast as her legs could carry her.

The Program Must Go On

A guy took Chani out and from the moment he picked her up at her house, he did not stop jabbering. He talked about anything—his car, his Mets tickets, his job, his goldfish, "Billy." He literally did not allow Chani a word in edgewise. After about two hours of his nonstop chattering and her complete silence, she piped in with one single sentence. He turned to her and said, "Thank you for that momentary interruption. We will now continue with our main program," and he continued right along where he had left off.

Jewelry To Share

Tamar had heard that her date wasn't so yeshivish. She was okay with that but was still shocked to discover when he showed up that he wore a chunky gold necklace on their date. Her mother had insisted she dress in traditional shidduch garb for her dates—namely a classic suit and pumps, and she was thrilled when her sister who had been standing guard at the window, yelled up to her, "Tamar, the guy's wearing a blue shirt, white slacks and get this—a necklace." Our little friend Tamar did a quick Superwoman change into something a bit more casual. In the end she told the shadchan, "He was such a nice guy, the necklace didn't even bother me." She added, "Hey—let's look at the bright side. If I marry him I could always borrow some of his jewelry."

So, my fellow readers, remember when reading these stories that dating is going to be an interesting journey. While you might never experience anything like one of the stories mentioned above (and you will probably be thanking your lucky stars for that), you will have to be versatile and ready to deal gracefully with unique situations that present themselves. Whatever curve ball gets thrown at you, you want to make it seem as if you are in total control of the situation and are completely unflustered. These stories are not intended to scare you, but rather to give you the confidence that even if you don't feel you have the ability to deal with whatever comes your way—trust me, *you do*!

Action Steps:

1. Expect the unexpected and be ready to deal gracefully with whatever comes your way.

2. However unusual your dating life might be, reading these stories (which are all true although the names have been changed) should help you realize that:

    a) your stories aren't that bad and

    b) if they are, it's important not to let it frustrate you but, rather, have a good laugh about it and move on.

MAKING
YOUR UNMARRIED
YEARS COUNT

While you are single, there is no better way to spend your time than broadening your horizons. Do not consider the time you spend dating and searching for the right person as time wasted! You can use this time to become more educated and well-rounded as well as learn about the Jewish world around you.

Now you have the opportunity to explore the walls outside your cozy house—see how Yiddishkeit is practiced throughout the globe. Get to know and understand your fellow Jews. Experience Shabbos at different families in various Jewish communities and solidify your idea of how *you* would like your family to be run one day. While you are searching for your bashert you can use this time to work at improving yourself and become the ultimate *kli* into which Hashem will pour the *bracha* so that you will find your soul mate.

I read a beautiful poem, quoted anonymously in a book *The Hundred Most Asked Questions About...Relationships* by Barbara De Angelo, Ph.D.:

"First I was dying to finish high school and start college
And then I was dying to finish college and start working
And then I was dying to marry and have children
And then I was dying for my kids to grow up
And then I was dying to retire
And now, I am dying,
And I suddenly realize, I forgot to live."

So, my friends—it's time to get out of your shell and live a little bit! It's time to trust in Hashem that your bashert will come in the proper time and place and grasp each day and not let it pass you by.

You may be thinking that you're not the get-up-and-go type. Perhaps you enjoy staying at home where it's comfortable and you don't have to expend any effort or act differently than you usually do. How are you ever going to meet people if you don't circulate? The deepest satisfaction in life comes when you exert effort. If you were handed a set of values from your parents and were told, "This is the way you are expected to behave," you are fortunate. However, one day you may have questions, such as: "Are these my beliefs? How do I find out for myself that this is the right path?" By learning more about yourself you'll be better able to know when you find someone who really is your bashert! By exploring Yiddishkeit and making Shabbos plans in different communities, you can get a better and deeper sense of why you are following the law code you were given.

There are hundreds of thousands of exciting frum Jews who can share with you their insights about Yiddishkeit, their knowledge about their Jewish past and ancestry

> **If you sit at home moping because you are not married you will never expand your horizons—nor will you meet your bashert or someone who may introduce you to your bashert.**

and their lifestyle. If you sit at home moping because you are not married you will never expand your horizons—nor will you meet your bashert or someone who may introduce you to your bashert.

I made a decision this year to spend one Shabbos of every month in another community, exploring how various families run their Shabbos tables and how Yiddishkeit is practiced throughout various Jewish neighborhoods. With just a metro card and twenty dollars you can spend Shabbos in Monsey, N.Y., Lakewood, N.J., Passaic, N.J., Riverdale, N.Y., Flatbush, N.Y., or Teaneck, N.J., just to name a few places. There are rabbis in all these communities who would love to have you and a friend for Shabbos and can set you up with people in the neighborhood for various meals. There is nothing like a Shabbos spent in the suburbs or in the city to revive you and give you renewed vigor to continue the week!

Had I stayed home, I would have never experienced anything like the incredible Shabbos I had once in Passaic, New

Jersey. The community was warm and inviting and just being away for the weekend did wonders for my spirits. We ate Shabbos lunch at a home where the woman was the most divine gourmet chef I have ever met. She prepared a spread fit for royalty—five side dishes, four meats and challah so fresh and sumptuous we finished three loaves in one meal. I picked up the recipe for the challah, as well as her recipe for carrot-crumb kugel, and pareve cheese-cake with French-vanilla coffee, which I have added to the repertoire of extraordinary recipes I plan to make for my family one day *I"H*.

She taught me the real definition of an *aishes chayil*. She was studying for a humanities degree while raising her five beautiful children, and still found time to prepare sumptuous meals and make sure her house was well cared for. What impressed me most was her cheery disposition. I watched with admiration as she made everyone around her feel comfortable and at ease. Watching her run her ship so smoothly, sparked in me a deep yearning to have a family of my own one day and create the warm, happy atmosphere that she has so successfully managed to build in her own home. Her husband is a professional; however, he sets aside time for learning every day and does not permit his children to watch television. Being with this family for the Shabbos meal taught me the importance of maintaining balance in one's life. One can be a professional, have a career, be a broad-minded person and *still* remain a G-d fearing Jew who makes Judaism the most important thing in one's life.

I am continually looking to improve myself, and make good use of my time while I am single. Recently, I came across a learning program in Israel at Neve Yerushalayim yeshiva, called *"pre-shalhevet"*—precisely the level of learning I was looking for. I was fortunate to have some time for myself this summer after I received my degree and before I started graduate school. I enrolled myself in the program eager to get back into the learning environment that I had been out of for so long.

> The Torah which the Jews received 3,300 years ago at Har Sinai is broad enough and sensitive enough to account for all the twists and turns that modern day society has taken.

Words are insufficient to describe what an incredible institution I found Neve to be. At first, I had thought that Neve was only for *baalot teshuva*. I soon discovered that they had recently opened a new learning program for people from Bais Yaakov schools who still feel the yearning to learn. Neve has some of the most talented and brilliant teachers in the world. One of my teachers was a former Harvard student and ski instructor. While he attended Harvard he randomly chose topics (i.e., anthropology, sociology, physics) and he would hole up in the Harvard library reading all the books he could on that topic. At one point, as he was studying all the various religions he came to Judaism. He was floored; here was a religion still in existence in the exact form that it had been practiced in its initial inception. The Torah, which guides and sets the foundation for our life today, is the very same Torah which the Jews received 3,300 years ago at Har Sinai. It is broad enough and sensitive enough to account for all the twists and turns that modern day society has taken. He continued studying about Judaism and before long became a *baal teshuva*. To hear him talk

> I watched rabbanim living what they preached ... we would watch the considerate, loving way they spoke to their wives.

about Judaism, and why it is the only right way, tripled and quadrupled my faith!

And every single teacher at Neve is like that; every teacher is 100% there for you—devoted to helping you grow and become the person you always wanted to be.

The lessons I learned at Neve were so profound—how can I ever describe them? I watched rabbanim living what they preached. They would lecture us on the importance of treating one's spouse with respect, and on Shabbos when we had our meals with them, we would watch the considerate, loving way they spoke to their wives. The rabbanim spoke of their wives as one would speak of the most precious gemstones. They understood that without their wife's undivided support and reassurance, their dreams to lead a family exclusively for the purpose of serving G-d would have evaporated.

After I left the summer learning program, I backpacked across Europe for a few weeks. While this is something that is loads of fun, it is usually not recommended once you get married, unless, of course, you marry someone who doesn't mind eating Tradition soups and bananas for three meals a day, in which case backpack away. However, this is something you definitely have to experience if you have the opportunity when you are single—if not for the purpose of seeing what Yiddishkeit is like outside of the convenience of a city, and how people manage in places where there aren't five pizza shops on one corner, then at least to see the beauty of G-d's world and be mesmerized by His spectacular universe.

What I found left a deeper impression on me than twenty novels about the beauty of Paris, Italy and Switzerland and a thousand lectures by people who have visited these places could have ever left on me. And I did this all on a student's budget—$800 and a backpack were all I had on me. In Switzerland I remember standing with my mouth gaping as I gazed at the majestic Alps—snow-capped even in August—and seeming to end where the sky began. In Italy, I learned to appreciate centuries-old architecture and discovered that, in many cases, modern architecture doesn't hold a candle to the old and regal. In Monaco, I watched thousands of people deposit their life savings into slot machines. I came away with the intense feeling that I would never reach a point in my life when I was so at a loss for things to do with my money that I would sit like a zombie hour after hour and deposit money into a slot machine. I wondered if the thought of giving this money to charity, education or social reform ever even entered these people's heads.

In Cannes, a small town on the French Riviera, I learned my most valuable lesson yet—never take your Yiddishkeit for granted. Although it is easy to practice Yiddishkeit in certain places, we must never forget how lucky we are and how so many people over the years have risked everything to light a menorah, bake matzos and even daven with a minyan just once. My friends and I ate *shalosh seudos* with a Chabad family that had been sent there on *shlichus*. The woman ran the mikvah and the husband ran the tiny shul nearby. I was completely awed by this woman raising her children in arguably one of the most decadent societies in existence today. At one point I actually entertained the thought that if I would ever have to move there with my family, I would make my children wear blindfolds when they walked outside. And she did all this just so that she could bring the message of Yiddishkeit to the Jews who lived there, however faint their *pintele yid* might be. As Shabbos drew to a close and her husband and children left to daven Maariv, my friends and I racked our brains to come up with a way to repay this woman for her hospitality. We decided to sing to her, "*Acheinu kol bais Yisrael hanesunim batsarah uvashivyah haomdim bein bayam uvein bayabashah*—Our brothers who are sitting in sorrow and in pain, who are standing uncertainly between the water and the high land, we are with you. G-d should have mercy on you." As the room grew dim, our soft, echoing voices lit up the house. I looked up and noticed the woman's eyes glistening with tears. I wondered when she last had heard religious people singing at her Shabbos table. We just wanted to return some of the *chizuk* and appreciation of who we are and from where we've come that she had given to us. She taught us the meaning of unrelenting commitment to Torah, regardless of what surroundings you were raised in, and how many obstacles stood in your way. We just wanted to give her something of ourselves to express our appreciation for her hospitality. The lessons I have learned, and the things I have seen—how could I have ever matched these experiences had I never ventured to leave my house?

But one can see G-d's wonders even closer—there's no need to cross the ocean. When I was at a wedding in Denver, Colorado I met someone who agreed to go skiing with me the next morning. Although I had never skied before I figured I had to grab this opportunity. Because she had a 4:30 p.m. plane to New York that same day she agreed to go with me only if we went to the ski resort closest to Denver (which was Loveland, approximately one hour away from Denver). The following morning we awoke at 5:30 a.m., and I drove and drove for what seemed to be forever toward the ski resort but there was no Loveland in sight.

I continued driving, growing more nervous by the minute. Two hours later I noticed a huge sign across the highway, "Welcome to Vail." Whoever imagined that I would get to see the famous town of Vail, Colorado. But I did—we did! In the end I discovered the reason we had never made it to Loveland—a gigantic snow heap had covered the sign. We skied at Vail for only a short time (because we had to leave at 1:30 p.m.) but nevertheless, the experience was exhilarating. I am a wretched skier so I initially went to the Bunny Hill. After two runs, I grew confident and thought to myself, "Hey, what's all the fuss about skiing in Vail—this is kid's stuff"—and immediately switched to the intermediate slopes. On one intermediate slope called, "free as a bird," I began gaining speed so quickly that I soon lost control of my skis and began heading directly into the forest. I forced myself to fall head first into the ski slope and sent my skis, poles, sun glasses, and hat flying in 150 directions across the mountain. After I got up and determined that I hadn't broken any important parts of my facial anatomy, I thought that maybe I would take it easy for a while and stop testing my limits. I gathered up my paraphernalia and crawled with all my ski stuff back up to the top of the mountain. I remembered I had placed a crisp, Macintosh apple in my coat pocket that morning before leaving for the slopes and I took it out now. I ate the delicious apple as I sat in the snow mesmerized by the mountains above me. All I can say is that I have never said a *brachah* on an apple with such *kavanah* in my life.

Sitting high up in the mountains is inspirational—it makes you think about humans, about G-d, about our purpose in this world, about why we were put here and what we have to accomplish. I realized that while I might be infinitesimally small compared to the enormous Rocky Mountains that loomed above me, nevertheless, G-d created me, and there must be a reason and a purpose to my existence. It is my job to discover what that purpose is.

If monetary reasons or other reasons hold you back from experiencing the world, I will add that even on a student's budget one can receive countless examples of how Yiddishkeit is practiced throughout the globe. There are so many great frum families out there with whom you can spend Shabbos. They will strengthen your determination to have a family of your own one day. Even if your own family is close to perfect, there are so many little things

> **Remember: The richer your life is, the richer you will be as a person and the more you can offer to a spouse and to your family.**

—like a father taking out the book, *The Little Midrash Says*, and asking questions of the children at the table, or a mother making the guests feel warm and welcome—that you might pick up on at someone else's house and say, "Hey, I like that, I want to incorporate that into my own home when I get married." Plus meeting different people will expand your opportunities to meet the guy or girl who will be that special one!

Remember: The richer your life is, the richer you will be as a person and the more you can offer to a spouse and your family. The more you see Yiddishkeit practiced in its ideal form and the more you learn about it from books—and, for me, from high mountains—the better able you are to serve G-d and appreciate the awesomeness of the world He has created.

Finally, there is also the added benefit that by doing these things and exploring your horizons you will become a more interesting person and you will find yourself with more to talk about on dates. Instead of the embarrassing lulls that sometimes accompany a typical date, you will now have an abundance of experiences, adventures and ideas on which to fall back. At a shiur by Rikki Cohen which I attended, a story was told of a guy and a girl who were going out for many months. One day, out of the blue, the guy gives Rikki a call. He says, "I've been dating this girl for months and I like her. However, I find that the dates are so boring—we simply have nothing to talk about." Rikki asked him, "What do you do during the week?" The young man replied, "On Monday nights I come home from work and I play nintendo. On Tuesday nights I play nintendo. On Wednesday nights I play nintendo. On Thursday nights I play nintendo. (Are you starting to sense a pattern here?) On Fridays night I daven and eat the Shabbos meal with my family and on Sunday nights I take the girl out on a date."

No wonder this guy was finding his dates boring! He simply had nothing to talk about with this girl apart from his score on NBA Jam—which, by the way, is not good date conversation. If he had thought to go to a shiur, pick up an enlightening book, read the newspaper, find a hobby, get out and discover what life was like outside of Sega country, he would have found many interesting things to discuss with this girl on their dates. If you make your life interesting and add exciting new dimensions to it, your dates will never be dull—you might have other difficulties—but you'll never run short on conversation.

I thank G-d a million times that I have been fortunate enough to experience all these different things. I have learned so much about life just from stepping out of my house, keeping an open mind and eagerly taking in everything around me.

Keep in mind, too, that one's bashert often is waiting for them to reach a certain level or potential before they can present themselves. It is my belief that you should do everything in your power to enrich your life and keep yourself growing and developing (this, by the way, will also keep you from moping).

Action Steps

When you want to be re-enthused with life:

1. Spend Shabbos with other families. This will help you decide how you want to run your family when you do get married.

2. Spending Shabbos with other families will allow you to make good use of your time and not allow the moments to slip by unaccounted for. In addition, it will enlarge the number of people who will be aware that you are single and looking and it will give you incredible, unduplicatable experiences that will enrich your life!

3. Traveling will make you feel lucky to be a committed Jew as you witness the wonders of G-d's creations and see how Jews everywhere struggle to keep their traditions.

AFTERWORD

recently received a poem in the mail from someone who had read my first book and I'd like to share it with you:

"In The End" by M. Bodek

Your dreams were dancing in the sky
  You thought you'd never land.
But soon you find it didn't go
  Exactly as you planned.
Then your eyes find a wondrous soul,
  Your hearts walk hand in hand.
And in the end.
  Yes in the end.
    Oh in the end...it's grand.

You find a soulmate in the end.
  Who brings you happiness.
But at the start you thought it ease
  Then found you were remiss.
For dating wasn't heavenly
  Nor was it cheerfulness.
But in the end.
  Yes in the end.
    Oh in the end...it's bliss.

Your hopes were soaring mighty high
  You thought they'd stand in line.
But soon you find it isn't so.
  But hey, you'll be just fine.
For dating, you thought, tasted sweet.
  But soured your lips like brine.
But in the end.
  Yes in the end.
    Oh in the end...it's wine.

You find a partner in the end.
  Whose soul reminds you of
The gentleness, the gracefulness,
  The sweetness of a dove.
Then suddenly you cherish
  All His blessings from above.
And in the end.

Yes in the end.
Oh in the end...it's love.

To my readers, I say one thing: remember shidduch dating is merely a bridge, a temporary transition to get us to where we ultimately want to go, namely married to a genuinely wonderful person with whom we can build a home.

While I am a big believer in dealing with a situation while it is on hand, (and that is why I persist in writing books on the topic of shidduchim) I maintain the firm belief that this stage, like every other stage in one's life, eventually comes to end. In the right time, and with the right person, the shidduch chapter will be completed and one will find somebody really special with whom to share their life.

It is my *brachah* to all of my single readers out there that they find someone like that very soon.

GLOSSARY

aishes chayil—woman of valor

aliyah—lit., going up; immigration to Israel

baal (sing.)**; baalei** (pl.)**; baalot teshuva** (fem. pl.)—a person from a non-observant background who has become religiously observant

bais medrash—house of learning and prayer

bas kol—heavenly voice

bashert (Yidd.)—one's predestined spouse

ben Torah—someone who lives a Torah way of life

beyidei shamayim—in the hands of G-d

bitachon—trust in G-d

bitul zeman—waste of time

bochorim—young unmarried men; the term usually refers to young men who study in a yeshivah

boruch Hashem (B"H)—thank G-d

brachah—a blessing, recited on food, special occasions, or when one fulfills a commandment

bris—circumcision

Chabad—Hebrew acronym for the Lubavitch group of chassidic Jews known for their involvement in outreach work

challah—braided loaves of bread made for Shabbos and holiday meals

chasid—strict follower

chavrusah—study partner

Chazal—our Sages

chesed—acts of kindness

chizuk—encouragement; strength

chupah—marriage canopy

cohen—a male of priestly descent

daven, davening (Yidd.)—pray, praying

d'var Torah, divrei Torah—lit., word(s) of Torah; a brief talk about a Torah topic

ezer kinegdo—helpmate

frum (Yidd.)—religiously observant

gemach—an organization that helps others through acts of kindness

gemarah—the Talmud

gornisht gehelfin (Yidd.)—for naught

halachah—Jewish law

Har Sinai—Mount Sinai

hishtadlus—personal effort

I"H (im yirtzeh Hashem)—G-d willing

kavanah—concentration

kishka—stuffed derma; food eaten at the Shabbos meal

kli—vessel

kollel—a seminary of advanced Torah study, which usually provides a salary for the married men enrolled

kugel—a traditional pudding-like cake, usually made of potatoes or noodles, served on Shabbos and holidays

letoeles—for a good purpose

loshon horah—lit., evil talk; slander

maaleh, maalos—good quality; good qualities

Maariv—evening prayer service

matzos—unleavened bread eaten on Pesach

mazal—luck

mazal tov—congratulations

menorah—an eight-branched candelabra lit on Chanukah

mentch (Yidd.)—lit., a man; but can be used for both males and females to refer to someone well-refined with good character traits

middos—character traits

mikvah—pool of water used for the ritual bathing and purification of people and utensils

minyan—a quorum of ten or more men required for congregational prayer and Torah reading

Mishlei—the Book of Proverbs

motzei Shabbos—Saturday night

nachas—pride; joy

neshamos—souls

parnassah—livelihood

pintele yid—Jewish spark

Pirkei Avos—Ethics of our Fathers

rabbanim—rabbis

rebbe—teacher

rebbetzin—rabbi's wife

red, redding—is suggested to; suggesting

shadchan gelt—money paid to the matchmaker

shadchan, shadchanim—matchmaker(s)

shaitel—wig

shalach manos—food packages sent to friends on Purim

shalosh seudos—the third Shabbos meal

shaliach—messenger

shidduch parshah—period of time when a person is dating

shidduch, shidduchim—matrimonial match(es)

shiur, shiurim—Torah lesson(s) or class(es)

shlichus—mission to help spread Judaism to estranged Jews

shpiel (Yidd.)—rigmarole

shtender (Yidd.)—a stand used to rest notes or books while studying or teaching

shul—synagogue; house of prayer

simchah, simchas—joyous events

streimel—fur trimmed hat worn by chassidic men on Shabbos and festivals

tachlis—a specific goal

talmid—student

tefillah—prayer

GLOSSARY

Tehillim—Psalms

tzaddik—righteous person

tzedakah—charity

tzniusdik—conforming to Jewish standards of modesty

yeshivah—an institute of learning, devoted primarily to Talmudic study.

yichus—ancestry

Yiddishkeit (Yidd.)—Judaism; a way of life adhering to G-d, the Torah, and rabbinic teachings

Yom Tov—Jewish holiday

zivug—soul mate